[handwritten: To Helen]

[handwritten: Best wishes]

Calendar Boy

by John Stirling

ISBN: 978-1-9163097-7-7

[handwritten signature: John Stirling]

To

Kay Lester and Sue Holderness

"Thank you so much"

Published By: -

i2i
PUBLISHING

i2i Publishing. Manchester.
www.i2ipublishing.co.uk

About the author

John Stirling was born into a theatrical family. Grandfather Edward Stirling was one of the great theatre managers; mother, Pamela Stirling was a film, theatre and television actress; and aunt, Monica Stirling was a best-selling novelist.

John kept the family tradition alive as a successful child actor and then, as an adult, preferring managerial roles, including writing, directing and producing for which he has won a number of awards.

For the stage, he wrote such musicals as *Once in a Lifetime, Gert and Daisy* and *Cheers Mrs Worthington*. His music productions range from Michel Le Grand and Sacha Distel to the Queen's Silver Jubilee concert. In television, his productions include *A Family at War, Wheeltapper and Shutters Social Club, The Comedians* and three *Royal Variety Shows*.

His Drury Lane charity concerts for special needs children were a hallmark. His annual Michael Elliot Trust Awards, where the profession honours its own, have become special nights.

A recent Grosvenor House concert, to celebrate Muffin the Mule's 60th Birthday, was a huge success. With John, you never know what's coming next.

John's latest work includes *Born in a Hamper* – Drama for theatre and television (touring). John Stirling is also a popular and sought-after after-dinner speaker with a number of prominent organisations.

Contents

October

November

December

8

Foreword

I am flattered to be asked to write the Foreword to *Calendar Boy* by John for whom I have the utmost respect, love and affection.

Over twenty-five years, we have worked together, enabling donkeys to have such a wonderful home, at the same time, making it possible for so many special needs children to benefit and achieve the impossible. It has always been a wondrous thing for me to be part of.

John and I have worked together as actress and producer and as president and chairman. We both hold mutual love and mutual friendship for each other, and I believe our perseverance and determination may have contributed to the success which the trust has undoubtedly had. Of course, things have not always been easy. In fact, many would have given up with all the setbacks that were placed in front of us while building this sanctuary, but I am so glad that we stuck at it.

My thoughts are also with Annie Stirling, who has supported her husband valiantly. When I consider dedication, I always think of Annie, who I admire so much.

The great thing about this charity is that, when you enter its portals, you find an atmosphere of well-being and affection from both sides, from the donkeys who seem so grateful, contented and happy to be there, and from the children happily working and living alongside their four-legged friends.

I hope you enjoy *Calendar Boy.* I have had the pleasure to play an active part in the productions of *Calendar Girls* at the Wyndhams Theatre in the West End and met the girls whose life we have enjoyed portraying, trying to imagine and give credence to their charity and the immense contribution they are still making to their cancer project. They went out on a limb. They too, persevered and showed great determination against much prejudice, until they eventually won through and created something very special, that is still today, contributing and financing sections of cancer research which are so vitally important to us all.

Sincerely

June Brown MBE

Prologue

What's in a title?

Having been kindly invited to undertake a tour of the Federation of Women's Institutes after an exhilarating audition in the Midlands, I had to think long and hard about a title to my talk, something relevant, something poignant and short that could trip off the tongue and more importantly, be remembered.

After much deliberation and thought, I came up with *Calendar Boy* believing this to be topical, relevant and right for the occasion, especially having seen the film, *Calendar Girls,* which portrayed a small group of women setting off with such courage on dangerous exhibition. Also, having many female actress friends and colleagues who have since taken part in the theatrical equivalent, on tours and in the West End to great acclaim, not only for their undisputed talent but also for their shapes and sizes, to monumental media coverage, I thought the title might be a winner and compliment all the hard work that had gone before me.

I was so impressed with the fortitude that the brave group of women from a North Yorkshire based WI displayed with imagination, creating what fast became a cult which was not only recognised as entertainment but went on to do exactly what it was intended to do and raise thousands of pounds for their hopes in achieving assistance in the research and cure of cancer. The fund has gone on to benefit the development of new techniques and drugs, along with so much else.

However, a fear came over me, one which I hadn't intended or considered. If my talk was to be called *Calendar Boy*, it might be misconstrued by groups of mature women with a maternal nature and disposition, mistaking the advance publicity with fear that I was not only going to talk but at some time reveal more than was necessary at their monthly meeting which had to date, been devoid of such specialised entertainment.

Being of a mature age myself and well into retirement mode, I was extremely and most definitely physically unable to pursue or perform the routines of a 'Chippendale' or even more worrying, the thought of this delicate and sensitive gathering of women having to sit through an amateur version of *The Full Monty* filled me with horror.

The thought that the ladies might have had an evening meal before leaving home to then be confronted by a gentleman of pensionable age revealing what can only be described as something he should be keeping very much to himself, might cause offense and irreversible indigestion, even worse, the imagination of others was of grave concern to me.

As my dear wife of fifty years explained to me without mincing her words in any way whatsoever, 'Darling, each year, bits fall off, even change shape to our detriment not for the better or for the faint-hearted. It would take a woman with a seriously short-sighted prognosis, cataracts or, at worse, having left her reading glasses at home, to enjoy that!'

I felt hurt but I knew exactly what she meant. I had not, in fairness, had any intention, desire or even courage to contemplate such an outcome, apart from being renowned for shyness and reservedness with the opposite sex, it would have been uncharacteristic and quite impossible at any cost.

After a great deal of thought, I decided the title of the book should remain the *Calendar Boy*. I would rename my talk, *Toytown to Buckingham Palace* which was, even though I say it myself, a wise choice, widely accepted as both prudent and sensible and has led to an exciting and affectionate liaison with the Federation of Women's Institutes who I adore and cherish at every meeting I go to.

Also, I felt that the title, *Toytown to Buckingham Palace* was an appropriate way to sum up my career in the world of theatre, music and television and the associated charity work that evolved out of it. These exploits went all the way back to when I was a child actor playing *Noddy* on stage to numerous other television, stage and film appearances. Moving on, I had become a writer under Jack Rosenthal working on programmes like *Coronation Street*. Later, I was fortunate to write, produce and direct in concerts, television and in the theatre with some marvellous stars including, June Brown MBE, Marti Caine, Patricia Hayes and others, as we shall see shortly, all of whom helped tremendously with the charity work of the Michael Elliot Trust and its Actors' Donkey Sanctuary, run by myself and my wife Annie for many years. In turn, this work not only saved many donkeys and provided wonderful experiences for disabled children with the animals but ultimately, led to a trip to Buckingham Palace and a meeting with the Queen. All of these special experiences led, ultimately, to my wonderful, productive and enjoyable association with the Women's Institutes around the country.

Indeed, at every Women's Institute where I make my talk, we have a party, so I dedicate this book to them, recounting some of the amusing, poignant and sometimes not so amusing anecdotes.

Chapter 1

The importance of women

I have always tried to analyse why, all my working life, I have concentrated my attentions on actresses for both help and reassurances in my work and its outcomes. As a writer and producer for the last forty years, my subject matters and my productions have always concentrated on the opposite sex, I have to add, ably supported by some of the best actors this country has to offer.

The attraction has not always been a traditional one as some of my most successful and moving works for both television and theatre have been headed by some of the greatest mature actresses, sometimes very unglamorously trying to face subjects ranging from poverty, care, abuse and other unpleasant situations the elderly have to accept and deal with.

I suppose I have had to hark back to my childhood for the answers I crave for, which give me the most satisfactory answers. I was brought up by two monumentally talented women, my mother and my grandmother. My father left when I was six and returned to his native France where he felt more at home. My mother, Pamela Stirling, was a very successful actress and in much demand for films and theatre, very beautiful and extremely talented in comedy as well as some of the toughest dramatic roles. Her early films of *Young Victoria* and *Saint Joan* became classics of their time. My grandmother, Margaret Vaughan, was equally famous for her acting ability and travelled relentlessly around fifty-seven countries all over the world promoting English theatre.

My grandmother was widowed as my grandfather, an actor of fifty-seven, passed away in Paris. She came to live with my mother and I in Chelsea which was a godsend for my mother who was always working, filming and away from home. My grandmother went on to chaperone me when it became my turn to tread the boards and perform as a child actor and finally, join the family business.

In 1980, my life was turned around by a woman who was unsure of her own strength and talent. I had written a musical concert, *Once in a Lifetime* which involved a leading lady being on stage for two hours surrounded by forty children of all ages and abilities, to perform sketches, musical numbers, dance routines and be funny at the same time. I had written it with one woman very much in mind, but it was going to be difficult to obtain her services as she was so busy and successful. It was also, not everybody's cup of tea, bearing in mind the actors' famous creed, 'Never work with children and animals.'

I chose Marti Caine's hometown of Sheffield which I knew she adored, and I was to choose all the children from the area to make her feel more at home and give her a real satisfaction that she had indeed, succeeded in coming home. I hired the City hall in the centre of Sheffield which seated two thousand six hundred as she had always wanted to perform there but she had never been given the opportunity. Now, all I had to do was to convince her that this was something completely different without frightening her. I tried to instil in her that the general public would not expect what she was about to undertake but that, at the same time, it would blow their minds.

Marti was appearing nearby at the Winding Wheel Theatre. It was a charity evening and the theatre was packed to the rafters. She gave a one woman show that, in my opinion and the obvious opinion of the audience, which was totally female, she was unique and outstanding. She was funny, she sang, she put across some somewhat risky material with eloquence and style and no-one could take objection to anything she was portraying. Everything she attempted made that audience love her even more. At the end of a gruelling hour and a half, she was clever enough to accept the night for what it was meant for. She gave a short but moving speech relating to her upbringing in Sheffield with parents who abandoned her and a grandfather who was less than kind over the years and often resorted to abuse and cruelty, it was a hard childhood but the way she interpreted it with such honesty in front of a large captivated audience was masterful. The women wanted to hear more of her early life and all that went with it in contrast to her success and what kept her going today. Marti proved to me and the Women's Institutes she was performing in front of, that she was indeed, a one off and that I could only consider presenting my show, *Once in a Lifetime,* if she consented to front it.

Marti was vulnerable and unsure of herself. Even though the adulation was there, she found it difficult to accept and deal with it, she would always believe there was a reason behind everything and that she was not equipped to deal with it. She believed that she would not be able to fill the City hall for a month's run twice daily and that although she was a local girl, she would not command the authority to front such a big show and to share the stage with forty children was mind blowing for her. Her fragility could not accept that she would make success of a situation like that. There was a strange lack of confidence which ignored the immense success she was having. But in the end, with the help of her strong and adamant manager, she accepted to take it on.

I then asked my talented wife Annie, to undertake the design and making of the wardrobe requirements so that I could present Marti with her vision of the style of the show which she did, and those designs and costumes blew everybody's minds.

I went to Marti's high-rise flat overlooking Sheffield and now put the finished proposition to her with as much under my arm and in my files that I could carry. She was charming, very shy and of course, the biggest hurdle remained in place, that she didn't think she could do it.

Marti stated mindfully that she was well out of her comfort zone. I assured her that I would work with the children until they dropped which worried her because who was going to work with her? We would rehearse at the Women's Institute in Sheffield for as long as it took and for as long as she could manage with all her other important fixtures.

The important ending to such a project was joy. The show itself was a huge success and not a seat was to be had for the whole run, many of the children who worked on stage with Marti have gone on to have successful careers themselves, something Marti would have been so proud of had she lived long enough to witness it. But that was not to be.

I am totally convinced, had Marti had the opportunity to live longer, she would have starred in *Calendar Girls* for sure, as in many ways, it was a piece written for her with her Yorkshire roots and her sense of adventure, she would have smashed it. She would have wanted to emulate what her Yorkshire sisters had managed to achieve as well as helping to raise the funds for the disease which finally and so brutally took her own life at such a young age.

Marti once came out with a wonderful quote;

'I don't want to have anything to do with donkeys. I married one and it didn't go as planned or even well!'

These words were both ironic and poignant considering that, as part of the work of the Michael Elliot Trust and the Actors' Donkey Sanctuary, Marti Caine went on to build the most beautiful eight-bedroom farmhouse for special needs children and their rescued donkeys in the village of Peak Forest in the Peak District National Park and not one day goes by when she is not mentioned or thought of.

I was also fortunate to work closely with Patricia Hayes, as we shall see, later in the book.

Also, another amazing woman I have had the pleasure of knowing and working with is June Brown MBE, a performer with an extensive career in film, theatre and television, who kindly agreed to write the foreword for this book.

The actor's philosophy has always been 'Never work with children or animals.' Fortunately, June Brown did not adhere to this ritual, for thirty years as president, making it possible for hundreds of children with special needs and their rescued friends to share an amazing trust.

June was honoured by the Queen for her tireless and enthusiastic work which so many children benefited from and where so many donkeys were rescued.

I am so grateful to June for writing the foreword at the beginning of this book.

Finally, a quick mention of Dame Judi Dench, a Vice President of the Michel Elliot Trust who, on hearing about my idea for a book, said;

'I find this a remarkable and amusing idea. I have always found John and his work fun and inspiring, and now here we have a record for our archives of just how good these times can be whatever situation he is in.'

Chapter 2

First, you've got to find them

There is no publication in this country, be it an atlas or a geographical magazine which can help you in any way find or discover the scout hut, the village hall, or any of the parish facilities laid aside for Women's Institute meetings. They are cleverly entrenched in secrecy or camouflaged to a high level that even the light infantry would have trouble pin-pointing their existence. Young, intelligent teenagers encompassing their Duke of Edinburgh Gold awards have failed their final survival test by not being able to uncover the whereabouts of the scout hut or hall shared with the Women's Institute. I have even heard from members of male Probus Societies with well conversed ex-RAF navigators say that they were unable to home in on them. I have thought of many systems that should be tried but not come up with anything the ladies think suitable.

To ask the president to wear an ankle tag on the given monthly day so she could be tracked, or asking the secretary or treasurer if they would comply with a chip implant number which could be tracked but the data protection being what it is today makes it impossible to contemplate!

There are no clues sometime as to be able to pin-point the actual village, the hamlet or the uninhabitable areas of countryside that house these groups, even barren surroundings which seem impenetrable must be found at some cost and must be located to make sure the select band of intrepid dedicated women receive the adequate speaker, whatever the cost to life and limb.

There is no satnav invented in the most modern car which will navigate directly to the obscure postcode which often turns out to be the programme secretary's residence. And which invariably finishes some miles away from a destination that does not register the unmarked lane or road, the prohibited farm track or bridle path which over the centuries have not been included in any ordinance survey maps, even well trained sniffer dogs would be completely baffled by some of the locations. Even the finest and most expensive compass needles don't move when required. And on the new roundabouts and carriageways which have been completed but not yet entered the satnav chain are there to send us all in the wrong direction.

I now leave an extra two hours on my journey or better still, travel the long distances to reconnoitre the area to find the venue to save me the state I get in or the nervous breakdowns I endure just before having to address the women for an hour. To arrive at last and probably only just in time, not only gives you the sense and confidence of an intrepid adventurer in the mould of Hillary and Scott, but it allows an insight into a wonderful charming dynasty nestling in some of the most beautiful parts of our country; places we would never have stepped into had we not been invited to do so by a WI group of wonderful women.

Sitting in a car park in an isolated location, surrounded by beautiful and rugged landscapes with no other habitat in sight, not even a streetlight, I am always thinking that I have made the most tragically bad navigational error and that this couldn't possibly be the right place. But there's the little car park we've all been waiting for, normally a Fiat 500 or a Fiesta, screeching past me and heading for the designated area and parking in the bay with the sign, 'President. Don't park here', not the expected land rover or tractor or any other four-wheel drive one would expect.

Suddenly, the lights of the hall go on, throwing light on the beautiful surroundings, the owl is disturbed from his tree and the place becomes alive. Within minutes, cars are pouring in from the surrounding areas, from hills and dales and very quickly, the actual hall is buzzing with activity. Chairs are positioned and trestle tables are put in position, an obviously well-rehearsed and tried routine they have been conducting for years.

One thing I have noticed several times in my journeys is that if I arrive early, it all goes better, they seem to associate the fact that you have found the place, or actually turned up, an advantage. I always feel when addressing such an assembly that I would be far better off listening to them, as their stories and adventures transmitted over wonderful mugs of tea and super Victoria sponge, are worthy of much notoriety and commendable episodes in quite outstanding circumstances.

They normally make you aware, if you have done well; if there's a chocolate digestive resting nonchalantly on your saucer or, a little tray is brought over with a lovely tea set with doyly and custard creams, that's a really good talk, as all the women have to make do with saucers that don't even match the cups.

But I am being unfair here, as I have had many wonderful and genuine comments and speeches of thanks which have even brought a tear to my wife, making her very emotional and grateful as it gives me that extra boost to go on to the next engagement.

After five hundred such engagements in just over two years to some of the finest groups, festival dinners, federation annual conferences and birthday celebrations, I always enjoy the meaningful reactions and the nostalgic comments the ladies find time to acknowledge with affection, it means a lot.

Chapter 3

President's speech

As the gavel shattered the air with three hefty blows on the table, the audience came to attention, on the fourth and final crack absolute silence reigned in the hall with eyes and ears facing front ready to accept the authority of the woman who had been installed in the position of leadership and control above all else and was to be heard and acknowledged as she stood above all in seniority.

"Good evening ladies. Will you please be upstanding for the start our meeting and evening together"

"Jerusalem"

"Thank you ladies, a resonant sound for the coming New Year if ever I heard one, but it does remind me that I must obtain the services of our piano tuner, it is simply unfair to expect Enid to battle like that every month to gain such an accomplished accompaniment. It is good to see so many members in attendance tonight as I believed the inclement weather and the past few days of festivities would keep the majority of you at home but I dare say like myself, an excuse to get out of the house for a few hours was welcomed with open arms

It is now that I must apologise to you all for the committee's decision to rescind our Christmas visit to the Theatre Royal this year and their pantomime, *Ali Baba and the Forty Thieves* which has received much acclaim. It was a move approved by the treasurer to save our finances for the coming year, but there comes a time when one must take responsibility and defeat at our error of judgement. Although with the very best intentions, we decided to support the local village hall's production of *Peter Pan*, an adventurous venture produced by our own local community and one we felt, or the committee felt, was worthy of our support. However appreciative of the initiatives and the amounts of hard work and rehearsals that went with it, the project seemed a little too adventurous, there was a good deal of appreciation when finally after many attempts, Peter actually got airborne and, it was noticeable that Cedric King was not a small, light young man. The technical efforts of getting him even a few feet above the ground where proving testing and, when he was unable to reach the height required to fly through the French windows of the Darlings' bedroom and found it impossible to make a plausible landing on their mantelpiece, the magic had fast disappeared. Some of the ladies mentioned they found the casting strange and to have our local girl guide leader as Captain Hook (without a hook) was testing, even though she did frighten the young children to death, it was not for the right reasons. I have, with much thought, already booked our seats for *Sleeping Beauty* at the Theatre Royal for next Christmas. Also, another apology for the complaints from some of you that there were no Christmas crackers at the Xmas do. It seemed to upset you and take away the season's greetings. Therefore, I have met with the treasurer and we have decided that we must adhere to protocol and not worry so much about penny pinching this year, I hope you agree?

Some of you have, hopefully, collected your newsletter and new badges at reception, so will have seen the highlights of last year's efforts and especially Mildred Thwaites' wonderful interpretation of Autumn at our last year's Harvest Festival. The photographs don't do justice to the size and strength of her magnificent vegetables and I can't honestly say her fruit display was outstanding, the size of the potatoes and courgettes were a revelation. Well done Mildred, real plus for our group.

Now I come to Denman College and Susan and Diane's journey to a day of work and interpretation which they both found interesting and fulfilling. Both have agreed to give you a full account of their adventure which I can't wait to hear.

Susan went into the sculpture class and spent a very full day making her first life sculpture in papier mache and glue, the subject being 'Adam and Eve'. She describes the instruction as extremely informative and I have to say, having seen the somewhat finished article, it seems an amazing to reach that standard in just a few hours. The couple in her work are most definitely male and female! And the positions they are holding are adequately sensitive to the image one expects of Adam and Eve. Susan tells me there are some refinements to be achieved at the next session, but she remains very proud of it, although apparently, her family do not feel it's ready for public consumption on the mantelpiece yet, we will keep you informed. Dianne, on the other hand, went into a crochet class and was given an exercise to make fifty-two squares six inches in diameter to make a bedspread, in the time allocated. Her instructor was very pleased and enthusiastic regarding her endeavours and although it finished the size of a tablecloth, the next session will put more meat onto the subject matter. We, as a group, continue our financial support of our wonderful college and its facilities.

There are three birthdays this month so would Celia Longford be upstanding for her card and potted plant with all our best wishes and many happy returns this month. Also, Evedney Carter, for her eightieth-year celebration which seems visually unacceptable along with her longstanding membership ranging for over forty wonderful years, her loyalty and affection held in great respect by us all.

I must apologise for being slightly late this evening for our meeting but as most of you are aware, I am a driving test inspector and I had three rather awkward women drivers who did not pass my requirements this afternoon and the last one decided to argue with me even though she had reversed twice into parked vehicles.

I must sadly broach the subject of our committee and its expectations. It is time to have some interest from you all for vacancies in our group. This year, we lose our treasurer, Colette who has given three of the most hard working years to keeping us in the black and allowing us to do things we never thought possible, also our programme secretary Elizabeth is going to live in New Zealand, so commuting is out of the question, you understand. Elizabeth has, over seven years, found some exciting and original speakers. She will be the first to admit that a couple have been classed as anaesthetics during their hour but overall, her record is flawless and a difficult pair of shoes to fit into. Finally, we have decided to appoint a kitchen manageress to oversee our tea and refreshment rotas etc, as we have some dinner ladies in our midst, I am confident they will breach the required gap and come forward. I was disappointed that no-one came forward at the last December meeting but now, we are in a new year with new values and meaningful forward plan.

I started off by wishing you all a happy New Year, heartfelt I assure you. I remain so grateful for your support and efforts. I mentioned I thought some of you would have probably made New Year resolutions, but we have to accept and appreciate the Federation too, will be issuing its own resolutions which we must consider, discuss and answer as a matter of some importance.

We welcome a new guest tonight in the hope that she will enjoy her time with us and perhaps consider joining us on a more permanent basis, also three guests from neighbouring groups who are most welcome. They are here as this year; it is our turn to present the annual get-together of the seven local groups with entertainment and suitable refreshments and listen with interest to their efforts having been made during the year. Elizabeth has already been able to acquire the services of Graham Walton, the father of sextuplets, who by all accounts is hilarious and most entertaining, something to look forward to!

Our tent at the local dog show raised over £120 which was marvellous. Mrs Huxley won, yet again, best of breed and pedigree champion with her basset hound which was expected as there were only three other candidates for the trophy, but the best cross breed class which was attended by the entire canine terrier cross sausage dog 'Summer' who won over all our hearts and minds attending.

It is with deep regret that I have to announce that Winifred Conor passed away at the Carlton care home at the age of one hundred and three playing whist with her friends. They expressed their condolences but were quite pleased as she was winning at the time as she always did but now leaving way for new talent to strive forward!

I will sign the record for the last meeting and our treasurer has left all the relevant information for you all to read at the reception desk. I need the prescriptions in by next month as we are rather low at present and I don't want to use the powers invested in me to drag the amount out of you!

At this point, I have to think about introducing tonight's speaker, from the title of his talk, I have no idea what it is going to be about, and I have to take Elizabeth's judgement that all will be well and interesting. He seemed pleasant enough when we spoke for a moment but who can tell?

So, without further ado, may I introduce, Jock Stribbling and his talk, *Toys Through The Ages*."

Chapter 4

January

Southam WI

Noddy in person

My first journey was difficult, the roads were completely blocked with traffic and a two-hour journey was taking three and a half hours. Fortunately, my wife Annie was acting as navigator. Aware that my nerves and our new satnav were not seeing eye to eye, both acting unreliably, she had wisely taken the helm. The road map was on her lap, but her directions were not filling me with confidence as Annie was having difficulty making sense of it all and I was already contemplating home!

After many detours and road diversions, a sign for Southam appeared out of the blue which gave us renewed hope that we were travelling in the right direction, but they were still the venue to find!

Stopping half the eligible voting members of the village, we were finally given some understandable directions and after twenty minutes, we glided through the secondary modern school gates and parked in the car park.

The car park was empty, the building locked but behind the car, the high hedge began to rustle and part in the middle and through it all, a lady appeared as if from nowhere, covered in leaves. She made her way down the side of the car as I wound down my window. I gave her my credentials and asked if I could go into the hall and set up for the evening talk. The voice was forcibly tough and had that edge to it as she explained that the meeting did not, in fact, start until 7.30 and she was aware it was now only 6.30, so we would have to wait an hour. She disappeared into the building.

Annie had made a welcome flask of latte and a couple of salmon muffins to keep us going so we tucked in, not feeling any sense of urgency. As I took a generous mouthful of salmon bun, there was a sharp tap on my window. I lowered the window and a lady loaded up with carrier bags, potted plants and other such things was glowering at me. I was instructed, in no uncertain terms, to follow her now. As I was unable to speak with my mouth full, I just did as I was told. This lady seemed quite formidable too. She introduced herself as the president of the Southam Women's Institute, a title I assumed held great importance and respect among her followers, wielding power and authority over all and sundry, a position bestowed upon her by revered colleagues and loyal supporters. But I was to learn later that nobody wanted the job and a replacement could not be found. However hard they tried; nobody was keen to follow in such a daunting task. But she seemed eminently conscientious as long as I was not going to take up too much of her time.

"What do you need?" she asked.

''Two trestle tables,'' I replied.

"Two!!!" she shouted back at me in disbelief.

This lady was not putting me at my ease, but I thought it best to remain quiet and just perhaps hope things would settle. I was also feeling a little tetchy as I was about to embark on a presentation which was untried and tested, an hour's show with props and large photos on easels etc, which we had worked out but only rehearsed in the privacy of our home.

I nervously asked her, "How many of you here tonight?" wishing and praying the answer would be around a dozen.

"There won't be many tonight as the weather will have put people off and to be truthful, nobody knew by the title of your talk, what it was about and that worries them somewhat."

At least that was welcome news and I relaxed a little, believing I would be able to manage that amount.

"Around a hundred and fifty," she said forcibly.

My knees buckled and Annie prepared to see me hit the ground.

Annie decided then and there that it was time to bring in the props and accessories to start setting up the talk mainly, she thought wisely, to take my mind off things, to look professional, as she put it.

The president immediately made sure she had the two biggest trestle tables and erected them in the centre of the floor which I thought indicated things were progressing in an orderly fashion and in my favour but she then produced an enormous sampler, embroidered with the group's insignias and threw it over the two tables. Out came the plants, the books, files for the evening address and all other matters relating to her welcoming speech, leaving me in no doubt that I was only a small part of the evening.

I found some courage from somewhere and asked, 'Where can I put my stuff?"

"Wherever you want," came a firm response.

"Sometimes, it's a bit difficult as some of our mature members can't hear very well, there's no microphone or anything so don't go far away, otherwise, they tend to shout out if they can't understand. There're not always considerate so it's best to just plough on. Otherwise, it can get a bit grizzly."

The news was being relayed that this was not going to be a walk in the park. Was it time to confess to Annie that my underlying thoughts were that we should go home? Maybe retirement was, in fact, the most sensible option at this stage in our lives? We had worked so hard to try and make this project entertaining, money had been spent on props, accessories, even visual effects, that it seemed shameful not to go through with it.

Now more women were entering the hall in single file, as the doors had just been opened, wet through, grumpy and displaying a sense of discontent that they should have stayed home. I thought that they were looking in my direction confirming that their decision to leave home was a mistake. Paranoia was setting in. Annie noticed my anxiety levels were rising, she placed a large carafe of water on the smaller table than required, as it was the only one left for us to use, she made everything look adequate and interesting, some of the women surrounded her as she worked, intrigued with what she was producing out of our flight box. Annie started to talk to them as she was working, answering their questions, both to reassure them that they were in good hands tonight and to give me some enthusiasm.

"They're really very nice ladies," she stated reassuringly, "It's all going to be fine."

The seal of approval from one of us was now established, for at least Annie looked as if she was going to attempt to enjoy herself and embellish our new project.

Eventually, as the evening progressed, the president finally rang her dinner bell to summon quiet and attention, cleared her throat and borrowed some water from my carafe. She had to ask several times for the ladies to settle as they had a long evening ahead of them. She started with messages of goodwill followed by a list of those who were absent that evening which seemed to be interminable; it seemed that half the village had ducked this outing; forthcoming trips which appeared by the reaction, to be a little too expensive for most; local walks of five to ten kilometres which seemed little too far for those with disabilities; the tea ladies' rota; the cake supplier; the treasurer's report; all the birthday greetings; a bunch of flowers for the ninetieth birthday celebration and to finish, a plaque for the longest member who had served the institute well over fifty years but who was not well enough to attend. Two quick choruses of *Jerusalem* followed, accompanied by a tape recorder which I hadn't seen in years and must surely class as an antique.

Taking this final chorus of *Jerusalem,* I stood in preparation to be announced.

"We will have our refreshment break now, I think," the president announced. "If the ladies would go and prepare."

I sat down reluctantly, looking at the wall clock which confirmed my thoughts that the president had talked far longer than I was going to be allowed to.

After half an hour, I was finally introduced by the president who had to refer to her notes to remember my name, even my existence and the title of the talk concluding with the important proviso that I bear in mind that the last bus leaves in forty five minutes and that quite a few ladies relied on its service!

I launched nervously into the first section. I could see Annie gesticulating to me to slow down a bit as some of it was being lost through the ridiculous speed, I was achieving so they could get their bus.

I opened, explaining my short stay at Sherbourne public boarding school at a very young age and that after only three months, I had been expelled. A look of horror was noticeable from a couple of elderly ladies in the front row who seemed to edge their seats back a bit, believing themselves now to be in some sort of danger. I was quick to reassure them that it was from nothing nasty and rather, that I was deemed by the teaching staff to be as 'thick as a plank' and that my mother's money would be better spent in a lesser academic establishment where more could be done to accommodate my lack of ability to learn anything. When I returned home, my father decided to send me to the Italia Conti Stage School because there was practically no schoolwork involved and I would be able in later life, to join the family business. In fact, I practically never saw the classroom as I was working from the age of nine onwards.

I recounted my first audition, having to face Enid Blyton who eventually chose me to play Noddy in her West End musical. I sensed at this point that I was getting a slight reaction from a somewhat damp and unappreciative crowd. I was now mentioning someone they recognised. I went on to speak of the show's success and as I was doing so, I was interrupted by a small, very energetic lady who, with great difficulty, had mounted her chair at the back of the hall, a feat which was making everyone around her quite nervous of the outcome. However, she seemed utterly determined to interrupt me in mid flow, waving her arms and shouting at me that she had something of great importance to impart to the assembled audience.

I noticed the president collapsing in disbelief that this could occur so early in my talk; that usually, speakers were allowed a little longer before being heckled in this manner. Again, she took a sip of my water carafe, now leaving little water if I needed it. Annie too, was looking fidgety, as the lady was now getting irate, insisting on being heard at any cost. I took matters into my own hands as the president left for the powder room.

"Madam, what can I do for you?"

I was clasping my hands tightly which could have presented itself as prayer which wasn't far from the truth in this case.

"You already have done," came a shrill but loud response from the back of the hall.

"I'm sorry madam, could you explain a little more to me?" I approached this with hopefully, enough feeling or constructive understanding, although I had absolutely no idea what was coming next.

"Yes," was a commanding response.

"You see, Mr Stirling, I have dementia. If I don't relay my thoughts to you now, I feel that what I have to say by the end of your talk, I may well have forgotten. What I have to say I believe to be important and relevant to what you are so entertainingly reporting to us that I hope you will forgive my intrusion but I hope also you will accept it as a compliment to you, so I must just tell you"

I was now nervous and completely out of my comfort zone. I was being placed out of sync with what I was going to say next and there were also a few worried faces appearing in the audience.

"Please continue," I said with fingers crossed behind my back. I have to say, by now, I was quite interested in what this little lady was going to come up with, so I just listened intently.

"In 1956, my mother and father took me to the Royal Court Theatre in Liverpool to see the musical

Noddy in Toyland. I had a bedroom full of posters of Noddy and all his friends and at eight, he was my idol. Noddy was very real to me. The show was a miracle, it was huge, with a large orchestra, red goblins flying all over the place, Big Ears and Silky the Pixie, all characters that I had come to adore in my fantasy of coloured books that meant so much to me. Now I was watching them live on stage, it was so exciting. Then, out of nowhere, Noddy appeared in his car with Mary Mouse in the boot and the audience went wild. The theatre erupted in joy. In the interval, my father had bought me a programme and unknown to me, I had the winning souvenir programme. My winning number was 29, the prize was to be announced at the end of the show, I still have it at home. My dad kept it as a surprise until the end of the show, then Noddy called out the winning number. Well, you can imagine my delight at hearing that. I am sure you will remember such things. If I can now, I'm sure you will be able to too. My life prize was a journey I shall never forget. You drove me around the stage and introduced me to all my beloved characters. Now you see, Mr Stirling, I can't actually remember what I had for my tea before coming out this evening but sometimes, out of nowhere, a flash back will be initiated, something sets off a response, a memory revived in an extraordinary manner, usually from way back, like school days etc. But sadly, for us, it very quickly disappears and soon must go back in that draw, sadly to stay there forever so, that's why I had to tell you now. I do remember that show where you were Noddy."

As the lady clambered down off her chair, I could see Annie was in tears and a lot of the ladies were very moved and accordingly, showed her how they felt by a very affectionate and loving response.

I didn't know how to get back to where I was before the interruption but the audience now helped me, after their rousing applause for their member and because of that heartfelt story, that wonderful moment in my eyes, I was able to gain their confidence and pick up where I had left off.

That lady's intervention that evening gave my talk authenticity, it brought me into their lives, it made us friends with a shared life so now, I carried on without worry in the knowledge that I must not let that lady down at any cost, she had done it for me as I hope I had been able to do it for her, all those years ago.

After I finished my talk relating to the Queen and our work in rescuing donkeys, I had to answer a lot of questions, but I left myself plenty of time to spend with my new-found friend from Toytown.

It was that night, my first night, that gave me the confidence to carry on, to realise that I did in fact have something worthwhile I could present that was interesting and entertaining. The first ordeal was over but there would be plenty more to come.

Chapter 5

February

Risley WI

Know your dialects

"You can't miss us, Mr Stirling. We are wedged between the Risley Remand Prison and Sainsburys. Look for the high concrete wall and high metal gate"

It was, in fact, not hard to find after such detailed directions, rather austere but nevertheless busy.

I parked outside in the place apparently reserved for speakers, or so it stated on the wall, but the president had had a recent hip replacement and it was the nearest space to the door, so I had to use the Sainsburys car park. This came in quite handy as I didn't have to use my trolley and made use of the big supermarket wheelie which took much more, and I was able to cross in two journeys instead of four.

I was welcomed by a charming grey-haired lady who welcomed us in a very friendly manner, announcing how all the women had been looking forward and waiting for my excellent talk on 'dialects'. Apparently, they had been using the month before my arrival to sharpen up and practice the dialects of the different counties for a quiz and competition they had on the subject. She lovingly showed me the competition table which was festooned by poems and song sheets from the different corners of our country, some she explained gleefully, had even learnt the poems off by heart in the respective dialects hoping for praise and perhaps, advice uncertain about whether to broach this subject.

I caught Annie's fixed and worried look and I thought for a ghastly moment that she might think I was going to try and take on this strange talk about which I knew absolutely nothing and that I would come out of it very badly indeed. Fortunately, I annulled her fears and went straight for the explanation to a lady who was now smiling at me in anticipation and making a joke in, what she assumed, was a real Lancashire accent.

"I'm afraid my talk has nothing to do with dialects. I am afraid there has been a mix up?"

"You are John Stirling?"

"Yes, I am, and this is my wife, Annie.'

"So, Annie does the dialects, does she?"

" No, I'm afraid neither of us do or would even be able to do a dialect."

"Well, may I ask what you do or talk about?"

"Toytown to Buckingham Palace."

"I see," she said, not being able to take things in.

"What's it all about?" she inquired.

"My life in the theatre as a child actor, then as a producer and finally, building a donkey sanctuary with theatrical friends," I replied.

"Oh, dear and can you not put in some dialects to liven it up a bit?" she asked.

"Not really and to be honest I don't think it needs livening up!" I responded.

"You may not think so, Mr Stirling but you haven't got to address a room with seventy women who have spent a long time working on this evening's theme, only to tell them they are going to hear about donkeys instead. It's not going to go down well and I fear that your reception might be blighted by such an announcement," she explained.

"Shall I go then?" I wondered aloud.

"That leaves me with no speaker, Mr Stirling and that wouldn't do."

"I have my confirmation note from your programme secretary," I said, producing the piece of paper and handing it to her.

"Ah well, I see what's happened here. The programme secretary changed halfway through the year and the new lady booked her own choice of speakers but hasn't registered properly. You are booked for July and that's months away," she explained."

I inquired, "What shall we do before we set out our props out etc?"

"Let me think a while, Mr Stirling. You see the dialect speaker may not be able to change dates and not be available to do any other dates," she continued.

"But she's not here!', I said.

"That is true, Mr Stirling and you are, so I am in dilemma as to what to do."

Trying to resolve things, I said, "I'll tell you what. I will set up and if she doesn't turn up, I will explain matters to the ladies, and we'll go from there."

"Easier said than done," she said. "But they can be very difficult if things are not well organised and the president can't leave in a hurry as she has just had both hips done."

As we stood wondering what to do next, the room started to fill with women. They seemed to be coming from everywhere and there were more than seventy as the 'dialects' title had caused a stir.

The ladies started to put their chairs out and settle, pulling out their bags, books and sheets of paper and conferring amongst themselves, sharing what they were going to contribute to the forthcoming evening.

My lady had now disappeared into the kitchen area and drawn the blind down.

There was now activity at the front door as many women rushed over to be of assistance to the president who had just arrived. It was rather like Cleopatra's arrival to Rome with some women even standing up as she came in.

The lady in the tearoom had now even turned the lights out in the kitchen and was not coming out.

As the president took her seat at the centre table behind the excellent sampler, she grabbed the microphone and welcomed all the ladies to their May meeting in what appeared to me to be a broad Birmingham dialect. She sounded rather like a character from *The Archers*. The ladies responded with lively applause and shouted out their welcome in various dialects.

Out of the window, I now saw my lady leaving the car park in her Fiat 500.

"May I ask, out of interest, Mr Stirling, which part of the country do you come from to give us a taste of what is to come?"

"Paris."

"France?"

"Yes."

"And yet, you specialise in our country's dialects?"

"No, I'm afraid I don't."

There was now some tension growing in the hall. The women were getting prepared for some sort of announcement.

"What do you talk about then?"

"My adventures and donkeys," I replied.

There followed a long silence, a very long silence as the president tried to understand the situation.

"And what is your talk called?"

"Toytown to Buckingham Palace."

"Well ladies, there seems to have been an error here and Felicity seems to have gone home early. What I suggest is that the tea ladies go into the kitchen and make tea and we will have our break while Mr Stirling and I iron this out.

Two ladies dashed into the kitchen, blinds went up and cups and saucers were thrown into place quickly in obeyance of the command.

"Well Mr Stirling. It seems the lady who was to have given us our delightful talk on dialects is not here so, I have to accept your talk," she addressed the now moaning and winging congregation.

"I'm sorry ladies. We have to accept what is in front of us, we have no choice. I have no idea what this gentleman is like nor what he is going to talk about, but my hands are tied. I will, of course, bring this up at the next committee meeting and I will expect answers, so have your tea and let's hope Mr Stirling lives up to something."

Mr Stirling did his hour accompanied as always, by his wife and they received a standing ovation. The president was eventually receiving admired reactions from his hardened and not always co-operative members with such quips as, "That was the best we have ever had!" So, the president was able to leave with dignity even though slowly but with dignity on her two sticks but unscathed by the whole experience.

The women, however, as they had found out from my talk that I was a theatre producer, wanted me to hear their dialects in the hope that I would find them true and entertaining. We obliged and we gave them each a smile and hope that if they worked very hard, by the time that the 'dialect' lady turned up, they would be perfect.

Chapter 6

March

Dunchurch WI

Dial 999

Thankfully, I was able to arrive early at Dunchurch WI, partly because, for once, the traffic had been kind. Secondly, the hall itself was prominent and visible from the A1. Mastering the Black Cat roundabout, I came to a gentle stop outside the front door and noticing a sign, 'Reserved for Speakers', I parked in my allocated spot.

The hall itself was surrounded by flat farmland and lush fields. A wooden sign proclaiming this was a public footpath was encouraging as we could now walk our tired and weary Cypriot terriers in the direction of grass and open spaces which to them, was most welcome. Summer, our bitch, was suffering from a nasty bout of cystitis and was in constant discomfort with it, in need of squat every so often. As my wife got the flask out and our lunch of sandwiches and sausage rolls from Greggs which I am partial to before a talk, I went off in the direction of farmland. I walked along gently as Summer, who was now sixteen with hind quarters not always doing what they were meant to, giving her the appearance of being drunk or dizzy. However, we enjoyed the air, the breeze was welcome as she sniffed every possible blade of grass, divot and fence post which I gathered had some interesting rabbit droppings on, not too common in Stockport but of enormous importance to her. After the fourth squat, I noticed blood, I took her straight back to the car and Annie.

"We must find a vet immediately," I said.

"What about the talk?" Annie replied.

"Well leave them a note that we'll be back in time," I assured her.

So much for arriving early!

It had been hard enough to get to the venue but now, in deepest Bedfordshire with which we were not totally acquainted, a vet had to be found and with no-one to ask. I drove straight to the Shell garage on the Black Cat roundabout. The attendant seemed quite jolly which was not the requirement and looked at me with a certain suspicion as I hadn't put any petrol in my car yet. He acknowledged my enquiry but had no knowledge of any veterinary establishment in Dunchurch.

'Try Bedford," he said with a smile.

It was an hour before we found the Bedford Dispensary for Sick Animals. They were excellent and saw Summer immediately sensing I was about to have a seizure if I couldn't return quickly to the hall. Summer was given antibiotics after a rather thorough investigation of her nether regions which she hadn't been keen on. But thankfully, she had refrained from taking the nurse's head off for which I was appreciative and that had gained her a reward from the vet's biscuit jar. It was explained to us that all should be well in four hours, as long as it wasn't her kidneys. The staff were extremely professional and kind which the bill emphasised, already the task had been spoken for in the way of remuneration. We made our way back to the hall with Summer sitting in her basket looking as if, by some miracle, she had been saved from a fate worse than death.

I got back still in plenty of time but with someone now having taken my parking space, the one allocated to me and no-one else. The front door was still locked, so I parked next to the offending driver and out came the flask and sausage rolls for another attempt at a coffee break. I had to share my sausage rolls as Summer was obviously feeling the benefit of her antibiotics, now insisting on some form of nutritional donation.

A man returned down the public footpath from a walk with his two chocolate Labradors, a little overweight but happy with the exercise they had been on. Summer was now relaxing in her new wicker basket having finished off three and a half sausage rolls, leaving me with digestive biscuit to go with my coffee. The man crossed the car park in the direction of the car next to me and called the dogs to heel. Both simultaneously took no notice whatsoever of the command and made a beeline for Summer and started unceremoniously investigating the nature of her gender. In fairness, the two of them had no idea of what she had just been through and the parts they were so interested in probably smelt of iodine and other such medications that had been used to quell the pain. A strange look came over them both but unfortunately, Summer took a defensive mode and she rounded on them, both teeth and nostrils at full thrust!

"She's very spirited," muttered the owner as he tried to get some sort of semblance of order watching both his dogs being mauled and humiliated by such a smaller bitch.

"She's feeling fragile," I said, trying to make light of the whole affair recounting to him at the same time the vet's work which had only been half an hour since.

Annie was able to relieve one of the dogs from a Cypriot terrier's grasp while the other just stood motionless astounded by the violence that had been inflicted on his partner. In their favour, neither fought back, just jumped into the boot of his car with their pride wounded but thankfully, still intact. Summer just got back into the reclining position she was enjoying before the intrusion and tried to hold the sausage rolls down. The man drove off with two sorry looking heads looking out of the back window while I quickly returned my car to its rightful place.

A small Skoda drove in and parked next to us. An attractive middle-aged lady wound her window down.

"You must be our speaker?"

I tried to answer with the digestive biscuit in my mouth, "That's right," said Annie.

"You found your own parking bay? I'm glad. It gets very busy when all the ladies arrive and some have to park on the road but as long as you're in and in the right place, everything's hunky dory. You have been highly recommended so they should all last the course!" she laughed. I tried to.

The lady got out of her car and walked towards the hall. She unlocked the door and disappeared inside. We finished our reduced picnic as we had time and I walked Summer a short distance around the car to check she had stopped bleeding, which pleasingly, was the case.

Cars started to arrive, and ladies started to accumulate in the car park carrying boxes, raffle prizes, flowers cakes and porcelain, second-hand books for the competition. I wondered if there was going to be time for my talk. No-one spoke assuming the car park sign was correct, and I was, in fact, their speaker, it seemed nothing more was required for them to know.

Annie and I set up the props and sales materials on two trestle tables, the whole thing looked very attractive and professional, all we had to do now was to wait for the ladies to have their short meeting, a quick couple of choruses of *Jerusalem* and we were off. The short meeting turned into a mammoth session with disputes and arguments and unpleasantness over no-one wanting to take over the secretary's post or the treasurer's post. After watching the way it was all going on, I could understand why they didn't want to get involved in these positions of authority but finally, after a cup of tea and a comfort break, they were ready for me. But was I ready for them? That was the question.

The proceedings started well, and I was into the first twenty minutes when the unexpected took place. A woman in the front row collapsed and started to gyrate and shake violently in front of me.

As two ladies came forward to assist the woman in distress, a voice announced with authority, "Would you please carry on, Mr Stirling, this happened before. If you would just carry on as if nothing has happened, we will carry her over to the radiators to keep her warm, we have already called the ambulance."

"Are you sure?" I said

"Yes, we are all enjoying your talk."

I looked over at Annie who was not only concerned for the lady but for me and whether this would affect my ability to carry on, even more, be amusing while the poor patient was in obvious trouble. She had by now, fainted and was out for the count, as the three women dragged her over to the wall and propped her up in a sitting position. I attempted to take control of the situation by carrying on. I had never thought of a situation like this occurring, so I was not in my comfort zone here. My instincts told me to sit down and wait for the ambulance to come and attend to the woman in question but, I did as I was told and entered a passage of the talk called for at this very time. I concentrated on the donkeys, the rescues and the special needs children and I must be grateful for the bulk of the large audience supported me and encouraged me.

After ten minutes, the medics arrived, one woman and her male partner, they were quite astonished to see me talking but by this time, the woman had been put in sitting position and had regained consciousness, she was a bit stronger but shaky.

I carried on as the medics went about their jobs; soundings, injections and a drip. They were very quick and thorough and had her in a wheelchair within minutes, so I regained my strength and got back into some more tales.

As I was trying to recount an amusing anecdote with a strong tag line, the male medic shouted out loud to the audience as if I wasn't even there, that it was not a stroke as suggested but the lady had not taken her insulin or her medication before coming out which had had an effect on her diabetes. The women all clapped and turned back to me as the wheelchair left the room. I had completely forgotten what I had been talking about but the kindly lady medic shouted out from the back of the hall, the anecdote I had been recounting, because she retorted, "I'm not leaving without knowing the ending to that story."

She got me back on track and I was able to have a quick glass of water.

I finished the talk and the ladies were appreciative or sympathetic, I couldn't quite gauge which. That, I thought, was the end of my day, but it wasn't.

As we left the venue, Annie decided to take Summer for her last stroll before setting off for home It was dark, and she tripped over a paving stone and broke her ankle. Just as the ambulance was leaving with our diabetes case, the back doors were flung open and this time, my wife was lifted in very carefully and then rushed to the hospital in Bedford sharing the ambulance with our recovering lady!

At the hospital, it turned out to be an extremely nasty break and requiring immediate surgery. As it turned out, it was a serious operation which took over four hours, but they got her ankle back in one piece with lots of bolts and screws. The Chinese surgeon was excellent in speed and the actual operation itself, which was quite intricate. I was so grateful as there had been five breaks to repair and rebuild. But within one week, my stoical wife was back on the road supporting me with a huge boot, making sure all was well and working.

We pass Dunchurch quite a lot on our travels as we have done many talks now in that area but we tend to go through it rather quickly, I always notice Annie sitting beside me in the car always tends to fidget and move her leg around in memory of our 999 night and even Summer seems to notice the night when the whole Stirling dynasty faced adversity.

I was later asked to go and do the Bedford Ambulance Medics' Christmas Party at Shefford which was a lovely night and there were our two medics who looked after all of us so well. It was great to see them again and I was able to tell her the end of the story she had not wanted to miss.

Sometime later, I received a lovely letter from Jennifer Pratt, Vice President of the Dunchurch and Thurlaston WI, thanking Annie and I for our efforts. Jennifer seemed reassured that the medics who had attended to everyone also had a good time. This letter can be read in full in the appendices at the end of the book.

Chapter 7

April

Brampton WI

Phoebe and Baz

It is twenty years since I was invited to talk to Brampton Women's Institute. I state talk because in those days as we had been operating the sanctuary for two years, my trips out were basically to inform and to introduce the trust to the public. I had not invented a talk as such, I was not booked as a speaker in those days.

Brampton village was wedged between Chesterfield and Bakewell. It had the most special needs units for miles around. The Ashgate Hospice dominated the proceedings but was flanked on either side by a special needs children's home, a centre for disabled children and a college for children with learning difficulties, so it was vitally important to us and our work to be known and associated with such a strong hold on care and special education.

The village hall was in the middle of the village and charming, very intimate and unassuming with a small membership of around twenty women, deceivingly modest for the work, this vibrant and active branch managed to achieve each year, always enthusiastic yearning to make life that little bit easier for those who so urgently required it to be so.

My first encounter was informal. We just sat around in a circle and I attempted to inform the ladies what we were trying to achieve, our objectives and taking questions from very informed ladies about disability and problems occurring from them. The respite some parents required being as important as the children themselves, always equating the patience required twenty-four hours a day in a caring for hyper-active and somewhat disturbed young people who need so much extra thought and care.

It was very much a living room talk but extremely helpful for us to hear from those in the middle of it all, how they handled things and how they dealt with it.

I was to learn one evening the ins and outs of Tupton School for Deaf Children, its work and care; what it needed for their special children in the way of visits and therapy; the Ashcroft School for the Blind and how the visually impaired kids benefited so much from outdoor activities which were not plentiful in the country at present; and through all that, my first meeting with Judy Dunlop, the Head Teacher at Ashcroft School, looking after forty children in need with so many various and intricate difficulties that needed special attention and care, at the end of my opening session I was able to invite

Judy to the trust to see for herself, to discover whether we could be of any use and if so, how?

The talk lasted a good two hours. We never deviated from the work ahead, the emphasis was clear and concise and revolved solely around the help that could be administered. The group of women were formidable in challenging all aspects of the problem with strength and determination.

I have always been so thankful that Brampton was the first and taught me so much in such a short period of time. It was now time to be constructive at what I had learnt, we had formulated a schedule of local assistance required and how we could help now. It was time to put it into practice.

The first chapter was to establish the relationship with the Chernobyl Children's Society in Derbyshire and to offer a home and holiday for young children who had suffered so much at the outcome of the nuclear disaster and blast in their country. They were overall, extremely unwell with leukaemia and cancers being the predominant illness and with little hope of recovery. The children had no experience or knowledge of country life. I was often caught unaware at their first reaction when coming into contact with a cow or a donkey and other such farm animals and their ability to overcome their tormented existence in response to an accident which they had no part in. Chernobyl was a tragedy for the innocent to bare and cope with, something that their elders and their countryfolk were not handling, with any fortitude or help, either medically or spiritually.

As the children came over, the Brampton ladies found suitable homes, attempting to keep them in pairs for, at the beginning, the available raised funds did not stretch to parents accompanying them, that was only to come later. They were all taken into families who worked hard to make them feel part of life over here. I was taken aback as to how long it took to get them over homesickness considering the conditions of Chernobyl itself.

It was always noticeable that the children arrived pale and drawn but after their month-long stay, there was a remarkable change and improvement in appearance, confidence and ability, personality and of course, their health.

The Brampton ladies made it their first task to see the children were seen by dentists who donated their services and their time for check-ups, fillings etc., they also made sure that they were seen by local doctors.

The women had a project where they bought each child a suitcase in which was placed things of tremendous value for when they went home: toothpaste, flannels, creams, towels, soap, t-shirts and underwear, having noticed there was a lack of such things on arrival. The women were also careful as they had been warned by those that knew that the children would be frisked on their return home for all the things that were unobtainable to most there.

Everything was given in triplicate to enable the children to share on their arrival home and to be able to retain the items meant for them.

We got on well with the kids, some were of an age that could manage to muck out and look after the donkeys and indeed ride as well. They were pleasant children with good manners, very polite, appreciative of the efforts made on their behalf on the whole, unaffected by the disastrous outcome that had befallen them. Understandably, there was certain hardness and strength of character at times, but we were very careful not to hinder that as they would require much of it intact for their return.

A month seems to go very quickly, there was a wish for longer, but the funds controlled the time allocated and the vital things that had to be accounted for.

We got lovely responses when the children got home as it seems the parents had been adamant that sincere thanks were necessary.

The Brampton ladies made this an annual happening. Many children have benefited from this initial drive to help. It is worth noting that many farmers and their children here suffered from the fallout from the Chernobyl disaster with acid rain falling at regular intervals and with the loss of sheep and cattle.

One of the ladies at one of our sessions mentioned in passing that she had been on holiday to Skiathos in Greece and that she had witnessed some horrible scenes involving donkeys and the way that they were treated. Unfortunately, I had taken Annie to this meeting unaware this subject was going to appear on the list. She listened and at the end of the session immediately high-jacked the lady in question and asked for more information.

To cut a long story short, flights were booked, the Brampton kennels accepted our dogs at short notice, and we flew to the Greek island. We booked two weeks, as it came under a package and it was much cheaper that way and believing there might just be time for a little sunbathing. After the two days it takes me to get my nerve back after a flight, we started our expedition to find the donkeys, which didn't take long as we just followed the overseas tourists and came upon the first group of eight small and emaciated beasts waiting patiently to carry a group of somewhat overweight holiday makers the six kilometres up to the monastery.

The heat was unbearable and to witness a small donkey with a weight of over fifteen stone on its back and having to climb a one-in-ten gradient was for Annie, impossible to watch. She lashed out at the owners and asked all the riders politely to dismount in order to give the animals another day of existence without hardship and cruelty.

This was met by a brutal response from the owners and guide who treated her to a barrage of language she fortunately could not understand but the meaning behind it was visible for all to see. The tourists did dismount in accordance with Annie's demands and in the knowledge that this practice did appear slightly mediaeval and an unnecessary part of their holiday enjoyment.

We were told back at the hotel the locals would be upset by this set to as it was the only means of employment and kept some families going and jobs would be lost.

One thing did happen on this beautiful island with its gorgeous stretches of beach and a harbour with fishing boats bobbing up and down alongside a wonderful sea front complex of restaurants and bars.

Annie decided she would spend one day on the beach. She chose one called Banana beach and went alone as I had meetings with officials trying to get a semblance of fairness in the way the animals could be dealt with in the future.

She walked a long way along the warm sands, paddling in the beautiful blue water with multi-coloured beach huts all along the way, people cooking fish straight from the sea and cocktails in abundance. One thing started to worry her as she strolled gently along the beach. It seemed to her that everybody around and passing her were naked, not a stitch on. She began to feel uncomfortable as she explained to me afterwards that, it seemed to her that it was all the middle aged gentlemen that insisted on demonstrating their prowess, trying to stop her and ask for the time or just trying to make conversation and making sure she was aware of their masculinity.

She said that had she herself stripped off and joined them they wouldn't have taken so much notice, but I was sorry I missed the photo opportunity of a lifetime!!!

When we returned home, Annie called some of the Brampton ladies to meeting at the trust. She showed the photos and images she had taken of the pitiful donkeys and the fact that she had not got all the way in making their lives easier, but she had an idea that she would, with their help, like to pursue.

Thus the ladies and Annie started their campaign in making fur girths and saddle rugs, bridles with linen inlays and sent over boxes and boxes over the years and when she actually holidayed there again, she was so thrilled to see they were all still being used and having the desired effect. The donkeys were still heaving their loads up the mountain, but the weights did seem considerably lighter and the officials had made two obligatory stops half-way up, with water troughs etc, which helped a bit, all was indeed, not wasted.

Judy Dunlop had become a regular visitor bringing her lovely bunch of children up and watching and marvelling at the progress many were making even with the need of callipers and some not being able to hear or see, but everyone benefiting under tremendously caring supervision and care.

It was to this end that Phoebe came into our lives. The last Saturday of every month was set aside for Phoebe, the bravest, most enjoyable young lady I have ever had the pleasure to spend time with.

When I saw the minibus arrive, I would put everything to one side and look forward to a couple of hours of sheer pleasure. The wheelchair was disembarked slowly and with care, the drip feeds were placed on the arms of the wheelchair and gently fixed into her system. She was usually covered in blankets with just her head appearing over the top, looking anxiously to see whether her best friend in all the world, Baz, was waiting for her.

We never brought Baz out until everything was ready for their encounter because due to infections and matters arising, we had to be cautious. Phoebe was always taken straight to the stables as that's where she most wanted to be as quickly as possible and the two would meet over the stable door at first, just to get reacquainted.

The muscular dystrophy meant that Phoebe was not able to move much, just hands and head and sadly, she was deteriorating as months went by, organs just seemed to diminish in strength and the doctors had warned the only thing now left where the lungs and then that would be the end. With all this to contend with, Phoebe was twelve years old, intelligent and extremely brave knowing everything that was about to occur and befall her and she was not fazed by the prospect, accepting bravely in a manner most would find unacceptable and impossible to contemplate.

As soon as she spotted Baz, that was it, the lights went on, she was able to embrace his appearance, show her affection and adulation, it has to be said over two years that this ritual was able to last, Baz himself was incredible. He showed very clearly that he was pleased to see her. He always showed her great affection and did a miraculous job. After a few minutes of introduction, he would be brought out of his stable and they would be able to spend or so of invaluable time together.

Together, they would have their picnic and Baz would never stray from her side, even though he was not attached to anything. When it came to say goodbye, there were long and heartfelt hugs and kisses and off she went in her minibus until, hopefully, next month.

A spur of the moment glance in the meat market at Chelford was to herald such a change in our lives and in the lives of so many children with special needs. This one animal would have so much determination, talent, personality and above all, intelligence, to build a trust and to share it with so many youngsters and fellow rescued donkeys, it was an outstanding achievement.

Baz made everyone feel secure. He wore the cross on his back and shoulders with pride. He never bore a grudge, his champagne ears and soft, full grey coat always in the need of attention and never short of young volunteers to fulfil the job.

Freshfields can never be the same without him, someone will invariably try to take his place as he has made that possible himself by leaving everything as it should be.

Love's last gift is remembrance and so it was that Brampton WI wanted Baz admired and remembered with a plaque for his tireless work with forty two special needs centres in and around Derbyshire with the Parkinson's Society, the stroke unit, the cancer commitment nationwide, the hospitals, the schools, the cathedrals and of course, the thousands of children he tended to for over twenty five hard working years.

Baz appeared on many television shows from songs of praise to the *Tweenies* from the *Terry Wogan Show* to *Coronation Street,* even *EastEnders* with his beloved June Brown MBE.

The Women's Institute of Brampton have always acknowledged this extraordinary donkey for all he did and stood for, giving so much hope faith and employment to all around him and just making things happen.

We loved him very much and we miss him terribly and we were lucky that the wildlife artist, Richard Whittlestone thought it necessary to commit him to canvas for all his work and joy. We now have a very beautiful portrait of him in our lounge that we look at every day.

To think that if we had not gone out of interest only to that meat market that day another half hour and that lot number which had been glued on his back would have meant the introduction to the slaughter house and he would have been sent along with the others to the Chum factory for dog meat, not only a miscarriage of justice but a waste beyond the imagination of many.

A short while later, I was to receive beautifully written, heartfelt but ultimately heart-breaking letter form Phoebe's carer, Emily. This letter was full of thanks for everything we had done for Phoebe on all her visits to the donkey sanctuary and all our efforts to ensure that she could enjoy those visits in the company of her friend, Baz. Sadly, the letter confirmed that dear Phoebe had succumbed to her condition and had passed away.

I made sure to reply on behalf of Annie and myself to assure her that we felt privileged to have been able to play even a small role in helping such a lovely child faced with such appalling circumstances. It was also our turn to be the bearer of sad news as we informed Emily of Baz's passing at the ripe age of thirty-seven.

I both mention these letters and have included both for the record in the appendices at the end of the book, not for any other reason that I believe the bravest children and the most patient and hardworking carers should be included and remembered for the work that they take on and the care they give which the Phoebe's of this world not only deserve but are so grateful for.

Chapter 8

April

Peak Forest WI

My favourite actress

One of my longest and most pleasurable associations and close friendships was with the actress Patricia Hayes. Our partnership lasted for over forty years in which time we played naughty children in *Ray's a Laugh* together on the radio. We starred together in a BBC series called *Charter Pilot*. I worked on the production of *Last of the Baskets* when she co-starred with Arthur Lowe and I finished up writing a play for her at the BBC called *Marked for Life* which in fact, created my charity later, The Michael Elliot Trust.

Patricia would come and visit my sanctuary in Derbyshire regularly as a patron, but she would always insist on staying in her camper van which she drove around everywhere. It was tiny but she loved it and she could take her three dachshunds around with her safely, it was very much their home too.

I was talking at the Brampton WI one evening and I do talk about Pat quite a lot. As I was doing so, a woman interrupted me asking me if I had ever stayed in her camper van with her. I explained it was far too small and she laughed.

"Why do you ask about that," I asked.

"Do you remember *Edna the Inebriate Woman*, Mr Stirling?"

I confirmed that it was one of Patricia's great triumphs for which she was awarded many accolades depicting an old down and out vagrant that no-one wanted to know. From this play, she was made the ambassador for the homeless, a job she took very seriously right up until she passed away.

"Yes, I do, one of her finest works."

"Well picture the scene, Mr Stirling, having watched the said *Edna the Inebriate Woman* two days before, I was asleep having gone to bed early with an early shift the next day when just after midnight, there's a tap at my front door, it was pouring with rain and I wasn't expecting anybody, so living alone I was nervous at opening the door at that time of night. I went down as the knocking carried on and I asked who was there. There was a muffled response, but I couldn't understand or comprehend what was being said so probably stupidly, I opened the door and there stood in front of me was Edna the Inebriate Woman holding a dachshund, drenched, in a dressing gown and with a torch. She asked me very politely if she could use my toilet as she had forgotten to go before, she got into her van. I just kept starring at her as if it was a complete dream having two days ago, seen her in this masterpiece. "Are you?" I asked stupidly.

"Yes, I am but still I need to go to the toilet like everyone else. Can you help me?"

"Of course," I agreed, she said and went on to expound how lovely Pat was. In fact, they broke open a bottle of Beaujolais and had an hour on the sofa before the little old lady left quite happily in search of her camper van which she had parked a short way down the lane. I just stood there for a while watching her make her way down the lane in total disbelief.

Chapter 9

April

Betchworth WI

To be or not to be?

I have always two great fears in my life in the entertainment industry and both emanate from my time as a child actor and the fragility and the responsibility hoisted on one at an early age, some would perhaps say too early. It has to be remembered that I started my television career at the age of ten and over the next seven years and over four hundred appearances in both TV comedy and quite large and intricate dramas, I was a nervous wreck.

You have to realise that in my day when our screens were still black, we were performing entirely live all the time. There were no recordings in those days, there was no going back and putting things right. It was very much a do or die situation and it was terrifying not only for oneself but for the actors one was working with. These were times of horror as everybody had to act on impulse and carry on whatever the situation.

Working in comedy with such lovely people as Jimmy Edwards who I played opposite in *Whack-o* for forty-two episodes over four years, I had to accept he was the master of ad libs. If he forgot anything, he could go into comedy routines well established over his long and successful variety career leaving at times, a boy to have to get us back to the actual story plot in hand!

So when I received a call from the Federation of Women's Institutes in Surrey asking if I would like to audition for them, the reminiscences of past auditions when one either got rejected which was disappointing, or accepted, which was terrifying came flooding back and those dreadful experiences facing a trestle table full of producers, directors and production staff which kept me awake at night returned to fuel my anxieties.

My argument at the time, as I had done a lot of good solid work, was why that couldn't be the catalyst for future employment and that's rather how it felt now as this lady was asking if I would like to go down. I explained that I had done over a couple of hundred WI's in the last two years and surely that could guarantee my credentials without having to journey down and have to prove myself all over again?

The woman on the phone was totally unimpressed with my pleas for clemency in the matter and my convictions that I was a well-known commodity and entity to the speakers' circuit did not cut any straw with her whatsoever.

"You do realise Mr Stirling that we have hundreds of speakers pleading with us every year for an opportunity to give a talk at our group meetings and that the ladies like to make their own choices, feeling that they have superior knowledge of what their members would prefer and enjoy."

I now understood that this was not going to be straightforward and that we were bathed in procedural business and that if I wasn't going to play ball, I was not going to be given any preferential treatment.

"How does it all work then?"

"Well Mr Stirling, we give each of our speakers ten minutes to give us a resume and a feel of their talk at which point, there is a bell which indicates that your time is up and that we have to move to the next speaker promptly."

"Just ten minutes to relay a lifetime's work?"

"I'm afraid so, Mr Stirling, we have a tight schedule and we like to be fair to all participants."

"And may I ask where you hold these auditions?"

"You may, Mr Stirling. We hold the day in Betchworth in Surrey in our village hall and you would be expected to be there for a 10.30 start in the morning."

I felt I needed to keep pressing the objectives and the rationale forward to this woman. "Do you not consider that ten minutes is a short period to recount sixty years of work etc?" But I was hitting a brick wall, it had become blatantly obvious that this lady was accustomed to the responses I was putting forward.

"It is not my position to consider anything, Mr Stirling, I am the speaker finder and it is my job to collect a number of hopefuls for our ladies to consider as to their suitability and even their ability to satisfy their members needs and wishes. After all, Mr Stirling, they know their groups and their likes and dislikes better than any of us!"

At this stage I was not going to give in and let her call me John!

"Seeing the distance, we have to travel, would you consider allowing us an afternoon slot to assist in our arrangements?"

"All the afternoon slots have gone, Mr Stirling, there is a high demand for places."

There was going to be no let-up in this situation and this well-rehearsed, pedantic woman was doing her job and obviously having to adhere to her Federation bosses and comply with their routines and demands. However, it was not an easy choice to make and we would just have to think it over.

I would have to discuss the matter with Annie and get her views and I was slowly preparing to dismantle my objections and fears of returning to those heady days of auditioning which I so loathed and which left me in such nervousness.

"Do I take it, Mr Stirling, you are not interested?"

Trying to be both polite and understanding at the same time was difficult.

"May I take your number and come back to you after I have had a chance to discuss this with my wife?"

A sharp response returned, "Don't leave it too long. I only have two slots to fill and I am under pressure to complete this by today."

The phone was then put down again abruptly.

Annie's look at the whole prospective was very different to mine, it took me rather by surprise. "We've only been doing this for twenty months. We want to make a good job of it and a success, don't we? Although I understand your reticence about auditioning, I do agree with your principle objection, but I think we should do just one and see how it goes or what it brings?"

Annie studied the road map and from our home in East Cheshire, it was two hundred and forty-three miles to Betchworth, they had made it quite clear that there would be no expenses. I would have to be ready and set up by ten-thirty in the morning which meant leaving before dawn. Feeding the dog early, making sure she had everything she required in the back of the car, Annie made flasks of coffee and breakfast rolls as there was little chance of stopping on this five-hour marathon.

Listening attentively to a neighbour whose life is spent driving up and down the country, the suggestion was that it would perhaps be advisable to drive through the night to avoid all the hold ups and diversions on the motorways. So, we fed the dog and set off after the ten o'clock news having waited for the weather forecast which thankfully was favourable.

We stopped three times, twice to let the dog out and once because I was no longer able to see where I was going.

We arrived finally at Betchworth at four in the morning, parked in the small adjoining car park and went to sleep with the dog on my lap who was still wondering what we were all doing still up at this time in the morning.

I awoke with a jump when car hooter blasted off behind me.

"You can't park there. It's the president's space, can't you read?"

Annie held me back believing if I was allowed to respond in my own way, we would forgo doing even the ten minutes we had tortuously driven down for. "Just move, darling."

As the pips went for the nine o'clock news on the car radio, the women started to appear in droves carrying boxes, potted plants, even what looked like dart boards

A lady struggled over the car park with an enormous tea urn, "Just for the committee love, they've had to get up early for this. They'll be wanting tea as soon as I get in."

I just looked across at Annie.

"Ten minutes, darling and all this will be over."

The other speakers started to arrive, mainly locals, some even on foot. They were all having trouble understanding why we had come such a long distance. One spoke out in honesty.

"If they actually like you, the fee never exceeds forty pounds."

I looked at Annie again, after all, she had decided on the expedition.

"Just do your ten minutes."

Eventually, the time came for me to do just that, my ten minutes was upon us.

I started quickly throwing in a few salvoes about Judi Dench and Morecambe and Wise to get their immediate attention as there was no time to waste here as, out of the corner of my eye, I could see the woman designated to keeping time. She was shining her large maritime bell with her glass' cloth, looking seriously keen to show the gathered crowd what a devastating noise and effect it could produce at the cost of each speaker if they were to dare to go over their allocated time. I had only done five minutes and she seemed to raise her gavel. I careered into another story as the audience were indicating their approval. I ploughed on and noticed the wall clock indicating that I was on my ninth minute, things were heating up, she was now practising her swing. But suddenly, the two women came forward and had a word with her, but she was adamantly sticking to her mandate of stopping the offender at all costs. Eventually, I could see the two women had removed her gavel from her hand and sat next to her defiantly and I was able to do fifteen minutes to loud applause and much joviality.

The woman returned to their seats leaving a very angry bell ringer jobless, the woman had even suffered the removal of the bell which had been reluctantly but forcefully placed on the floor in front of her, making the whole issue a humiliating disaster on something she had been required and volunteered to do with her best ability as a professional and dedicated member of long serving. I had to feel a certain sorrow but combined with admiration for those who had forgone all privileges for some time to come.

It has to be said that the women who defended my right to conclude properly were well aware that they were now in serious trouble; that they would be reported to the committee for their bravery and ill-advised assistance and would need a solid explanation. I felt, if necessary, I would be prepared to travel down, at my own expense to witness and defend if the case came to the Federation for review.

We didn't wait to see the other speakers but hopefully something came from it for them to, as we left the car park, homeward bound, we were allowed the pleasure of hearing what the bell actually sounded like as some poor unfortunate speaker had overstated his welcome and received what I had to admit was a devastatingly loud maritime bell which was obviously made to warn shipping of imminent disasters in the channel. The woman had finally got her way.

When we got home, there were many requests on our answering machine to go down and talk to Surrey groups, over the weekend. We finished up with over fifty bookings in all.

The imminent success of our trip to Betchworth was that I had to offer Annie a three-course meal at her favourite fish restaurant.

Chapter 10

April

Great Bookham WI

The Bookham Belles

My first engagement emanating from my brief audition in Betchworth was an invitation from the Bookham Belles at their venue, the Manor House, Bookham, Surrey.

After a five hour journey, we arrived close to our destination but unfortunately, the British road authorities, in their infinite wisdom, had neglected to inform the nation officially that it was just completing a new major roundabout on the outskirts of the village of Great Bookham itself, meaning that our trusty satnav had not yet been updated with the news and was in turmoil, trying to find a way through. All navigational aid was not functioning and any aid to furnish a professional and smooth glide into our destination was in grave trouble. They had installed half a dozen diversions which all seemed to end back at the roundabout at which we had a holiday route avoiding the village of Great Bookham the exact spot we were aiming for. We travelled through Small Bookham, Bookham West, Lower Bookham and to end our journey, even Higher Bookham, where we finally found a local garage owner who although fed up to the gills with half the nation asking him how to get to their destination, finally gave us detailed directions and we reached Great Bookham for which, we will always be eternally grateful.

One could only be impressed as we drove up the short meticulously manicured lawns and hedges. Then we got our first sight of the manor house school set in a Capability Brown design with a classically built Queen Anne house in formal gardens and parklands of exquisite beauty, tucked away in a surprisingly quiet and leafy corner of Surrey. Many speak of it being the right place for the 'Quiet Girls!' with the school excelling at building confidence that certainly becomes apparent in their opulent surroundings. "Our girl was never the one to put her hand up in class, yet now she's form captain," that's the motto and states the obvious.

I assumed quite wrongly, as usual, that I was going to be entertaining a small group of mature ladies with a long association with a valued and well-respected institution. I assumed they had worked together as land girls, but this manor house school, established in 1920, with the aim of developing happy young women who believe in their ability and achieve their personal best at all times, didn't yet fit with my premise of nostalgic memories and lives laden down with the history and decades of work and toil.

Entering the hall, it was clear that it was being well preserved and looked after in keeping with its grandeur, the character and momentum of the house was intact for all to see and admire. The remarkable thing for me was that it had been taken in hand for the benefit of the young and that they were all so conscious of their heritage. It would appear it was in very safe hands at present.

The lovely winding staircase up to the classrooms was excellent, registering taste immediately. There were only twelve desks in each classroom inviting the thought of individual tuition at its best. Stunning bay windows overlooked the immaculate lawns. The rectory transformed into an elegant dining room when required to do so. It was all a joy to see as we walked through to the assembly hall where the headmistress finally took her leave by introducing me to the president of the Bookham Belles.

I was immediately taken aback as I was expecting a matronly figure who would be so in keeping with our surroundings but in one moment, Sally wiped away all my premonitions as she stood in front of me, hand of welcome outstretched.

In my travels around the country to Women's Institutes, I had formed my perception of what a president looked like and I became quite good at recognising the said person without them even being introduced to me but now, this was not what I had expected.

Sally was young and extremely attractive, vibrant and enthusiastic seemingly about all matters relating to her official status, obviously delighted with the authority bestowed on her and proud of the achievements she had been allowed to make. She was ready, it would seem, to put across new ideas at the drop of a hat, inject a modern slant to her institute without in any way losing any of the standard practices and goals that she recognised only too well as sacred and worshipped in a new light, all this came flooding across in the first fifteen minutes of our introduction.

The Bookham Belles were now arriving in droves and even Annie was astonished, reminded of her days at the London Palladium when she climbed to the top of the theatre to have coffee with the Tiller Girls in their dressing room. The Belles were youthful, they bought with them anticipation of a good night ahead of us, a lively evening was promised as I learnt they had all researched Annie and I on their laptops before coming out!

Immediately, I felt at home and Annie settled into some nice and constructive comments with a few of them. Although they were youthful in thought and spirit, quite a few had obviously been past students at the school, and they were now in good jobs so that their children could now benefit. As they conversed over a welcoming glass of Chablis, Annie and I gathered they were expecting something out of the ordinary, I felt now it would be tragic if I couldn't live up to their expectations.

I noticed in the front row, a lady sitting next to a young man who looked slightly out of place in this female domain, in fact it was not hard to notice him as he was very tall and no-one wisely had sat directly behind him but rather found comfort three rows back as their view would have been completely obscured.

Being the only man in the hundred-strong ensemble, I was careful how I reacted to his presence. Not wanting to make him feel too awkward in an already difficult situation, I did not want either to embarrass him in any way, but he was outnumbered.

"Good evening, Ladies and Gentleman," putting the focus on him straight away, I thought I would clear the air.

"I am delighted to see you here tonight, but I have to ask whether you are, in fact, in the right room or in what capacity do we have the honour of your presence? Perhaps you thought there might be others of your own age surrounding you." (To which the women reacted with groans and whistles.)

The young man thankfully was well up for all of this, he stood immediately radiating confidence and accepting the accolade given to him by the woman. He seemed unperturbed by everything, even the wolf whistles that were showering down on him because I have to admit, he was very sleek with the latest hair-style, very smartly turned out becoming of an evening out with ladies, no socks and trendy loafers, looking every inch the part being a total credit and asset to the Belles who were obviously fond of him.

He spoke with an assurance unusual in one so young especially in the company of so many women, but he seemed to have had some experience.

"My mother was interested in your publicity hand out especially that you yourself had trained at the Italia Conti Stage School in London. I am myself at the school and when I mentioned that you were coming to talk to my mother's WI, my headmistress suggested I should come along and report back to the school afterwards as to what the evening was like, support of one of the old boys, as it were!

As he sat down, I made him stand up again.

"Have you been at the school long?"

"Five years," came the reply.

"Knowing the school well, you will have had many jobs now?"

"I have finished a season at the National Theatre in a play called *Chips with Everything* by Arnold Wesker," here, we both smiled at each other.

"Yes, I know you were in that play too, but we didn't play the same part. I have had a small part in *Coronation Street*," again, we met each other's eyes.

"Yes, I know you have directed that, and I am about to embark on a national tour of *Stop the world I want to get off*."

"Perhaps the time has already come for me to sit down and let you take over?"

"Not really, Mr Stirling. I have already entertained these ladies." He sat down to more applause.

"You do realise I'm sure that the wonderful musical you're about to tour was written and performed by Anthony Newly after he left the Italia Conti Stage School? He was my prefect and what a talent. I do hope you get some inspiration from his work and I am truly delighted to think you are going to keep his wonderful work alive around the country, if you come up North, Annie and I will definitely try and come and see you, good luck."

That was enough and we had both covered our ground and I now had to get into my talk.

He stood up again which I was not expecting.

"I thought you might like to know you have already done yourself no harm this evening as my mother is the treasurer and you may not have to argue now too much over your fee at the end!"

He took his bow.

I have to admit I was slightly concerned seeing that the women were younger and that they might not recognise all the characters, actors and actresses I was going to talk about but I need not have worried as they recognised all of them which was a huge relief. Of course, when it came to Billy Fury and the Beatles, it took me some time to calm them down, it nearly got out of hand with what they said they would have done with them given half a chance. The perception of upper class and affluent living standards suddenly vanished to working class hysteria and fun. I did explain that one of my jobs was to collect some of the lingerie, bras and knickers thrown at the boys during the evening's entertainment and had to try and get the clothing etc., back to whom they belonged as most of them were lathering at the stage door waiting for a glimpse or a touch!!

"It's no wonder Billy Fury was so shy at what state you're all in now."

The whole evening went really well. A fine audience, a fun crowd and a very appreciative gathering which was not only boosted my confidence but gave me the courage to go forward to various types of audiences over the country because I had found the response awe inspiring.

Annie was quick to point out, "There you are. There's the ten minutes you nearly buggered up and didn't want to."

We drove home after the talk, adrenalin kept me going the five hours although in my excitement, I forgot the dog was in the back. We returned through Little Bookham, Small Bookham, Higher Bookham and at Bookham West, I had to let the dog out for a pee. This time we didn't mind the holiday route which added an extra hour to our journey, it was now worth it.

The satnav and I were no longer on speaker terms as Annie had unusually fallen asleep with the dog snoring on her shoulder. The satnav was unable to cope with all the roadworks and diversions on the two major motorways I must have driven a hundred miles out of my way, in the end, I had to wake Annie and get her on the job as the dog was now showing signs of incontinence!

To this day, the Bookham Belles remain such a happy memory. I am now always keeping my eyes and ears to the ground to see how the young man survives in this turbulent profession. He did get very good notices in *Stop the world, I want to get off* and Annie and I were very impressed when we saw him in it at the Palace Theatre in Manchester and he seemed genuinely pleased to see after his performance.

I was sent this leaflet recently and I think it is important information for the Women's Institutes in general;

'Due to overwhelming interest in Bookham Belles WI, we now have a full membership and we have a waiting list. When Bookham Belles started in 2014, we had such a fantastic response that there were enough on our waiting list to form another WI, so came about the birth of the Bookham Butterflies, the volume of demand to join the Butterflies made it necessary to form the Bookham Bees. Seeing that all three WI's are already holding waiting lists, a mutual decision has been made that to be fair to the women who wish to join a WI and do not have a place, no dual membership between these three WI's will be permitted. In other words, new members must decide which of the three afore mentioned Bookham WI's they wish to join."

Well done girls. We can't wait to come back and meet the Butterflies, the Bees etc.

I also became aware of a nice summary of my talk communicated in a newsletter written by the president of the Bookham Belles, again which can be found in the appendices, at the end of the book.

Chapter 11

April

Waddington WI

Beethoven

A blue canvass of cloudless sky, the swallows had returned and were circling the barns for insects. Preparing their mud nests for their young arrivals. The return of the swallows heralded that Easter was upon us, I was separating the bills and brown envelopes from the more ominously pleasant white ones when a rather larger than average one stood out.

On opening the envelope, I took out a very beautiful Easter card which had obviously taken much more time to paint and put together with pictures of wildflowers and a collage of petals with real pressed flowers which made it very special.

"Happy Easter to you, your wife and all the donkeys. Best wishes, Ruth and Bill Seed, Waddington WI."

Immediately, I wanted to thank the participants and found the WI number in my book and eventually got hold of Ruth and was able to thank her personally. She was very pleasant on the phone telling me how much she had enjoyed coming to our sanctuary a couple of times and spending days with the donkeys. "A real treat in today's world," she said. "May I ask you whether you would consider bringing a donkey to our village for our Palm Sunday celebration, we have never had one present, it has been a dream of ours, our group decided this was the year we must really try."

The voice was meek and mild, rather vulnerable, as she wondered whether she had overstepped the mark or asked too much. Immediately, I put her at her ease. I was only too pleased that she requested such a thing, even though life was about to become difficult having to get the trailer out and choosing a donkey that would be suitable to visit a small Lancashire village church. I told her I would get in touch when I had chosen the donkey and organised myself. I decided it was my duty to try after all, the trouble she had been to also, I have to admit, that I looked forward to celebrating that special day in that special way, so I agreed.

"That's wonderful," she said. "Would it be asking too much if you could bring Beethoven?"

What a choice. The only stallion in the herd, the tallest and strongest we have in our midst but very handsome and strangely very co-operative at special occasions and gatherings, indeed quite converse with days out. "Okay," I said. Beethoven it is.

The lady sounded pleased, as if she had been triumphant in her successfully accomplished mission and organised achievement which could give her extra status within the group, no-one having been able to come up with anything similar over the years.

Beethoven is at least reliable, very gentle and easy to get on with as long as there are no lady donkeys around when things can become quite different. He then tends to show his other side but on reflection, I had to admit, he had a good record of public appearances under his belt apart from one outing to Ripon Cathedral on a Palm Sunday mass when we cantered around the cathedral uncontrollably rendering a packed congregation and the archbishop concerned for the safety of his flock. The worshippers became rather stupefied and nervous at the speed Beethoven had reached in circling the cathedral due entirely to the cathedral's stone floors which made the sound of his hooves echo and reverberate which frightened him. The faster he went, the louder the hooves. The dean eventually caught him after four laps of the vast cathedral but had to be seated quickly as he showed signs of a cardiac arrest.

In Manchester Cathedral, the archbishop of Manchester informed us that we would be doing a pilgrimage before the mass through the streets of the city, leading a cross-bearing clergy plus the full boys' church choir before entering the cathedral for the actual mass. The actress and president of my trust, June Brown, was in charge of Beethoven that day, leading him through Manchester but unfortunately not at quite the same speed as the cross-bearing clergy and choir boys. In fact, within a very short space of time, he was nearly a mile in front, showing no signs of slowing down, June Brown having just celebrated her eight-second birthday shortly before and being renowned for her intake of sixty cigarettes a day, was struggling, finding him hard to keep up with and feeling rather lonely, walking alone through the Mancunian thoroughfares with the very faint voices of the choir some half mile behind. But the enthusiasm of the crowds spurred Beethoven forward and they arrived at the steps of the cathedral a good ten minutes before the procession!

At Liverpool Cathedral, Beethoven excelled himself. I think it was basically the pomp and circumstance of the event which got to him, the heraldic trumpets as we went in, the sound of the massive organ just freaked him out, mesmerised him, made him feel the sense of occasion, the importance of it all, he was now centre stage just where he wanted to be or even though in his own way, he should be. He was brilliant and the archbishop was even able to make a joke as Beethoven brayed loudly twice during his Easter sermon, the archbishop commenting that it sounded right.

In keeping with the occasion which received a gentle ripple from a packed cathedral, he got away with a very special homage to the lord on his day!

So now, here we were both again at the Palm Sunday but this time, at a lovely, small, well-kept Lancashire beauty spot, its babbling brook alongside the beautiful coronation gardens which have earned Waddington 'Best Village in Lancashire', on many occasions. I explained to Beethoven that Henry VI had lived in the village for twelve months at Waddington Hall before he was betrayed by the Yorkists, but Beethoven didn't seem bothered.

The stream was high, running fast and the banks covered in daffodils which Beethoven seemed interested to devour. Villagers sat outside in the two cafes watching our arrival. I held him tight with the lead rope round my waist in case he decided it was time to explore a little more adventurously. If Beethoven wanted to go to the right there was very little I could do about it, except call out for help!

Beethoven made his mission to mow the well-manicured grass verges on the way up to the church, I feared the consequences of such action in a small intimate Catholic centrally-heated church, but I prayed hard that Beethoven would hold it all until afterwards. I asked him gently with deep conviction to let me know if the circumstances arose to want to relieve himself, just to let me know or at least give me a clue. He never had done it before but there's always a first time for everything in life.

Inside the church, it was delightful, full of charm, flowers in abundance, the interior had been transformed to accommodate the occasion, rays of sun hitting the pews and warming a very full congregation who all stood as Beethoven walked in (he loved that). A nice touch I thought and by the look of Beethoven holding his head up high, ears erect and very much looking the part, he was registering well with the audience, who were all smiling, some delighted that he had actually turned up.

We took our place as we had been instructed to at the side of the altar rails by the stairs leading up to the pulpit. We fitted perfectly. Father Almand came forward. He welcomed everyone and publicly blessed Beethoven by touching his ear with a drop of incense which made the animal a little uneasy due to the fact that Beethoven bears his name because like the composer, he is deaf, that being the reason he travels so well because noises can't disturb him. Father Almand was not to know that and I didn't feel it was the time to go into lengthy explanations.

I was busy preparing my thoughts for my talk 'A Small Miracle', when I happened to notice the whole church had just recently had a beautiful red carpet laid throughout at obviously, an enormous expense. With all the grass and flowers, Beethoven had consumed, I could be facing a hefty dry-cleaning bill, that is, if they could remove the stains. The only answer was for me to keep a very tight hold on him, at any signs of fidgeting or unease, to whisk him out of the side door, which was close to us, marked 'Fire Exit'.

Father Almand came over to me having incensed the whole church now and invited me to climb the winding staircase into the pulpit to address the congregation. He explained the verger would stand and hold Beethoven.

I could not refuse in front of an intimate but very attentive crowd, so I nervously handed over the lead rain to the verger who seemed to take control adequately. As I climbed the stairs up to the pulpit, Beethoven didn't take his eyes off me until I went out of his vision. He couldn't see me as I was directly above him. I started my address 'A Small Miracle' about an orphan who lost his parents in World War Two and finished up living alone in the compounds of the Basilica of Saint Francis in Assisi. It is sad but a meaningful and beautifully written account of a young boy and his only friend, his donkey Violetta, the way their lives intermingle and how they completely relied on each other until one day, the donkey falls seriously ill. It is a somewhat sad account of the young boy's determination to make things right. He fights hard for an audience with the Pope so that they might knock down some walls in Saint Francis' Basilica to get Violetta down to the crypt so he could help her recover. I could see some tissues coming out but Father Almand seemed pleased with the outcome, encouraging me to carry on which I did until I heard Beethoven below, rapping his hoof on the floor. He was beginning to get unsettled with the situation of having to stand still. I spoke now very loudly so he could hear me, I was close by, but this was not a great comfort to him, he now wanted to come up himself into the small pulpit which would not have taken the strain. I sped up the talk, tried to edge nearer the staircase so he could actually see me and we finished up meeting halfway which seemed to satisfy his anxieties. We both finished off the address almost together with the verger now having attached the lead rain masterfully to the pulpit staircase.

I was so relieved that I had got through my story and I came down in a rather clumsy manner, but Beethoven was there to save me, as always. As the choir boys gave a beautiful rendition of an Easter hymn, I relaxed foolishly and took my eye off the ball which allowed Beethoven to eat a full display of flowers that had taken the WI some time and a great deal of effort to put together. He was now full of flowers as well as everything else he had devoured on his way in. Signs of fidgeting were now apparent. I got him out just in time although the welcome mat at the front of the church would need an overhaul. I was pleased and relived the red carpet had remained intact and immaculate. Even the whole impact of the incense was not going to get rid of this in an instant and, as the congregation left the church, there were some remarks that just had to be accepted.

I find this last item uneasy to relate to you all adequately, as it was very much a personal experience, a very strange feeling, one that I have not felt or experienced before. Somehow this small intimate church, the occasion for which we were all gathered; Beethoven being by my side; the general atmosphere of an ecclesiastical experience very accurate in its beliefs; a sympathetic service with no frills but devoting itself very much to what it must be focussing on, seemed to make me feel in keeping with the occasion, glad that I had been allowed worship in these surroundings with my donkey and this congregation. I heard my Grandmother who I adored when she was alive say things to me which I could not comprehend properly but I was able to get the gist of it. Just knowing she was there that day meant we had both kept in touch through means neither of us were ever going to be able to justify or explain to each other ever again.

This small church in Waddington has stayed in my memory for years after we visited it. I am returning to Waddington's Women's Institute next year; I am really looking forward to that. I am hoping the church will be open as I have always wanted to pray in there as I never got the chance before. I suppose the atmosphere will be different and not anything like the occasion we went through, they do always say it's a mistake to go back somewhere after a meaningful visit or experience. But Beethoven died last year at the age of forty-eight and having worked with thousands of special needs children and having attended so many glorious occasions, he was a very special donkey. He was a stallion for part of his life with me so I have been able to name his foal Waddington and who knows, I may well be able to take him to the village where his father made such an impact and gave me an experience I will never forget.

Chapter 12

April

North Yorkshire WI

A woman of substance

Small and diminutive she may be but determined and capable are the attributes that I attach and are more relevant and in keeping with this dynamic organiser for the North Yorkshire West Federation of the Women's Institutes. Forthright and straightforward are only two of the attributes that label some of her abilities. Determination and honesty stand side-by-side with her approach to everything asked of her.

When I was attempting to put together a coast-to-coast walk involving five children and their five donkeys, I could not find a way to get the project off the ground. It was a 347-mile walk and my estimate was a schedule of three weeks, as the children were between the ages of eleven and thirteen years-old. Annie was to lead the walk with her sister Linda in support.

The first and most anxious commitment I was making for the children and the animals was that of safety, a responsibility that lay solidly on my shoulders. This was to be a hard trek for so young a party. The parents had accepted their children's participation, all being well and properly organised. On that basis, they had agreed that their offspring could attempt the daunting task. In fact, their attitude was that the achievement, if well managed, would give the girls extra confidence and gain them some strength from doing something of this nature but for it to work, the children had to complete the task, otherwise all the effort and sacrifice would be in vain.

First, Annie and I went up to Scarborough and started the walk from the beach, aiming to reach Blackpool beach in as long as it took for us to get there.

Halfway through our walk, we stopped at Ripon and I used the opportunity to call at the headquarters of the North Yorkshire West Federation of Women's Institutes to see the chairman. We had a coffee and in the conversation regarding some talks that I was going to do, before leaving, I managed to explain why Annie and I were in Ripon, relating our attempt to get the five children across the country with their donkeys.

I explained that the children had themselves, asked to do this adventure and I was attempting to put it all together with all the problems that went with it, including all the health and safety implications and also, that it was turning out to be a nightmare.

The chairman was extremely helpful explaining that although the WI could not get involved in the charitable side of the walk due to restrictions in their mandate, she felt that she could perhaps advise and point me in the right direction.

"I understand that you are talking to our group meeting at the Georgian Theatre in Richmond, next week? May I suggest that after your talk, you make yourself known to our North West organiser, Jo Kearns, who will be there in her capacity as programme organiser. Jo is very easy to get on with but above all, totally capable of helping in a situation like this. Knowing her as I do, she will want very much to get involved. Her work with children in this area is acknowledged as second-to-none and she loves animals and a house full."

I thanked the chairman and we set off on our way to Lancashire. We reached Blackpool in eight days but decided that with the age of the girls and the donkeys, due to their capability and the need for safety, that it would take them twice as long.

The Georgian Theatre in Richmond was overwhelmingly beautiful. It was a historical piece of early theatre with small inside seating of around a hundred and thirty people with a balcony right around the auditorium. The stage was deep but narrow with free-standing wings of historical importance. To stand centre stage, facing an intimate audience, was just something special. Being from a theatrical background, it meant a lot to me to be there, I was just blown away with the uniqueness of the venue. Certainly, the opportunity of being able to enjoy the experience was dear to me.

The evening went well, and the WI had organised wine and cheese in the foyer afterwards. It was there that I met Jo Kearns for the first time. She had organised the evening.

"A daunting task, Mr Stirling?" she said with a smile.

"Yes," I said, "Not one to be taken lightly."

"The chairman has explained the basics to me, and I agree that the safety and welfare of both the kids and the donkeys must come first. You not only have the worry of the children's safety but on top of that, you have the animals to care for too. I imagine them both to be of equal importance to you?"

"Absolutely," I agreed.

"I have estimated that the actual walk will take around three weeks, as I believe that thirteen miles a day is sufficient for both children and donkeys to manage in comfort. Even that will be hard, day after day for eleven and twelve-year-olds, and it will mean no days off."

"I hadn't worked that out yet," I admitted.

" There is also the question of the donkeys who will need places of rest along the route with safe and quiet paddocks which must be arranged at the same time. I have put a map together for you and I have marked every village on the route which has a working WI that I think would be willing, in fact, very happy, to help. The children will need some attention in this quarter. I feel that good meals at night and a hot bath in a comfortable homely set-up is what will be required. Hopefully, I will be able to arrange properties in the farming community who will have the necessary requirement for animals. This will have a safer prospect than putting the animals on open grassland away from everybody. It has to be remembered, Mr Stirling, that donkeys, especially in good condition, are vulnerable to theft, so security is of utmost importance for both. Would you agree?"

I certainly would have agreed if I hadn't been so taken aback by all the work that she had already put into the project, including all the thoroughness of her disclosures and thoughts. With us only having met each other for the first time, immediately, I felt totally in safe hands, desperately grateful that this outstanding woman was going to help in such a professional and knowledgeable way.

"What can I say?", I asked.

"Nothing," she said, "It's your venture, it's an attractive adventure, one which will also maintain a high profile for the organisation. It's a project I feel will benefit the children and animals well. I have always believed in therapy and the combination of these two elements working together deserves our attention. I am glad to be of help and hopefully, a small part of its success, all being well. With your agreement, I will start to check out the groups the women and their homes. Okay?"

"Very okay," I said, and Annie just couldn't help herself and gave Jo an enormous hug well in keeping what this lovely lady was doing voluntarily and so capably.

Within a month, I received a schedule of houses that the children would be staying at, thirty-three in all. Each one had acceptable stables, barns or paddocks for the donkeys. The WI's of each accommodating village had also been instructed to put together a coffee morning to see the group off to the next village.

"You will have to work out for yourself along the route where you are going to stop and eat and have appropriate breaks because those have to be decided on-the-hoof. But I will put a list together of the facilities and cafes in some of the local towns and villages. I am now off to Lancashire, Mr Stirling, to meet with the Lancashire Federation, as my job is fundamentally over when you reach Goosnargh and it then becomes the responsibility of the Lancashire groups, if they are agreeable to help."

"Are you sure, Mrs Kearns?" I asked, genuinely concerned that it was a lot for her to take on alone.

"I may find the time difficult, but I have the inclination. The desire is that we see this project to a safe and successful conclusion. One task I must ask you to sort out which I cannot do, is to check the actual conditions on the roads and perhaps, the need for police presence to be looking out for you at certain vantage points in towns and villages, to make sure that the transport authorities and police are totally aware and conversant with your whereabouts at all times. Can you do that for me?"

"Consider it done," I assured her.

I was suddenly made aware of how much organisation it must have taken Jo to do what she was doing because dealing with the transport police and traffic people was a nightmare. There were mountains of paperwork and forms to return and as soon as I mentioned what we were intending to do, I had weeks of negotiating with people who were putting every obstacle you can imagine in our way to make things either impossible or difficult. But eventually, between us, we got it organised. It was now left for Annie to train the children and donkeys to walk thirteen miles a day relentlessly for the required time of the walk. It took her three and a half months in weekends, to get everybody, including herself and her sister, equipped for such an ordeal.

I spent the allocated time dealing with the children's health checks, with replacing their school absence with tutors and schools when the girls were on the road, which they would have to attend one day a week. The donkeys also required health checks and the farriers had to make the donkeys fit for purpose, especially their hooves.

Eventually, the day arrived when we all made the journey in our horsebox to Scarborough, all the children in the back, sharing the space with their donkeys to keep everybody calm and affectionate towards each other.

Jo was at the Nicholas Hotel on the seafront at Scarborough to meet everybody. This was her first sight of the children and their proteges and she looked delighted and moved as she watched them alight from the horsebox.

There were a couple of local photographers taking some shots as we took the donkeys to their field, high on the hill, overlooking the resort.

We all spent the night in the hotel which had been donated to give the girls a good start in the morning.

The beach at Scarborough was quite full of spectators which I was surprised at, but Jo had again done a good job of informing everyone, there was even a band. The council had brought their own group of beach donkeys to say goodbye to their friends and they were giving rides on the beach which our own animals found amusing and tried to join in with. The beach operator told me the lovely story about how one night, the beach donkeys got out of the field at the outskirts of the town and everybody thought they had escaped and were never going to be seen again but there, in the early morning, were the donkeys on the beach in their usual circle waiting to give their first rides. I think that answers the question as to whether they like what they do on the beach every day. The natural affinity to children is clear for all to see.

Alan Ayckbourn, the town's celebrity playwright and theatre owner, came down from his house to the beach to see everybody off in style and soon, it became time to set off for our first destination, the village of Stainton.

I have to say, at this point, it would be difficult to relate every village and what they did for us over the three weeks but enough to say that Jo Kearns had achieved something quite remarkable. All the children arrived in Blackpool with no blisters, no problems, no fall outs and seemingly very happy at their journey and success.

The donkeys on other hand, had been, at times, a pain in the backside, always pulling for the verges for grass, sometimes refusing to go forward as requested, often giving us a hard time with cars and heavy traffic and determined to rest where they saw fit rather than our designated stop areas.

At Blackpool, we had to reach the town hall where the Lord Mayor was waiting, to welcome the party and to invite them into the town hall for tea and cakes.

The mayor seemed delighted to see the children and presented them with a gift from the town. The next morning was Sunday and the Pleasure Beach was to be closed for the morning, so the girls and their donkeys could have the place to themselves. They could go on anything they wanted, eat anything they fancied, the place was theirs for four hours and everything was fully staffed.

The children were very excited but had decided off their own backs that they couldn't accept this generous offer unless Jo Kearns and the thirty-three ladies from all the villages that had helped them were there too.

So it was, that Jo had to quickly arrange a coach from Scarborough to cross from coast to coast, picking up all the ladies to bring them to the children at the Pleasure Beach the following morning. She did it.

The youngest lady on the coach was in her early eighties, she was having a birthday that week. When the women arrived, tired after their long journey, the children showed them no mercy whatsoever.

Straight onto the Big Dipper followed by the Space Odyssey, shooting up into the air over Blackpool followed by the Ghost Train, the Revolving Cups and Saucers and the Racehorses. No-one went to the pick a duck or bingo stalls which the women were looking forward to. The food was not to every woman's taste and included doughnuts with piles of sugar, burgers and ice cream which were the order of the day with a huge candy floss to finish.

Jo came over to me, as I had done my best to disassociate from the group as I simply don't have the stomach for all the things that were going on.

"I've been told by the Yorkshire coach driver that I'll probably need an ambulance to take the women home after this," she informed me.

"Are they in a bad way," I asked.

"Well," she said pensively," some have been sick in the waste paper baskets but I have noticed them sitting on benches with the kids on their laps smiling and joking with each other, so I am assuming I will have the same number to take back as I brought."

I had to now say what I had been waiting to say for a long time as meaningfully as I could without embarrassing her.

"You've been unbelievable Jo. None of this could have been done or even thought of without all of your dedicated work. The children owe you so much, as we all do. I have been astounded by your skills, your talent, your determination to see something safely through to its end. I can't thank you enough."

Jo was embarrassed but Annie and I hugged her, and the parents had all bought her things, for seeing everybody so safely and successfully across the country.

Jo Kearns is a woman of substance, a woman who wishes to do things for others, she wishes to help and endeavours to make as many lives as she can that bit more acceptable and happier. Surely that must be what the Women's Institutes stand for and to me, she is one of their greatest ambassadors.

Due to the organisation, the determination and courage of Annie, Linda, the five girls and their five donkeys, the coast-to-coast walk was well received and managed to raise £26,000 for both children's causes and donkey sanctuaries.

Some years have passed now, and the children still keep in touch with the women who were so kind and generous to them. Some, of course, are no longer with us but still held in very much respect and fondness.

For me, I have tried very hard to get hold of Jo Kearns. I have been given e-mail and addresses but with no joy yet. I know her dear husband passed away, but I am hoping that we will be put in touch with each other again one day, even if it's in a very different place and environment. God bless, Jo.

Chapter 13

May

Lytham St. Annes WI

The last resort

Sitting in a new, beautifully designed shelter, framed between two piers, the North Pier on my right and the South Pier on my left in a glass dome having been newly erected to promote the brilliant new promenade, I was able to relax.

Facing the Irish sea, rippling in on a moderate breeze, what could be better, the gulls circling and screeching, waiting for the next opportunity to dive bomb an unsuspecting child or adult for the contents of their ice cream or even better, the fish and chip remnants in that evening's local paper. The extravagantly refurbished golden mile was opening a history of memories and events for me, like opening a scrap book, on every page, a near forgotten thought or reminiscence.

I have always held the town of Blackpool with great affection and respect. I have, however, never had the courage or the inclination to climb to the top of the tower but that has never stopped me from admiring it. My wife just nips up at every opportunity as she shows no fear or nervousness at such an ascent, but I have always been able to accept my seriously strong adverse reaction to the heights. My wife will always insist on describing in graphic detail, the view from the top and, when she stands on the glass floor with nothing between her and the promenade below, she seems to enjoy watching me disintegrate with signs of impending nausea.

Many people have lost their virginity in the resort having participated in a naughty weekend but all I have lost in this overwhelmingly exciting fun factory are my teeth. At the time, I didn't think I was being naughty rather that the Fylde Council hadn't quite got to grips with levelling off a few prominent paving slabs, one which gave a valiant paramedic overtime trying to find and retrieve my entire top set of really well-kept teeth. This was time that he could have spent answering more serious cases instead of having to crawl around on all fours picking up teeth and placing them in a glass of milk for the nearest dentist to deal with it. It all took time as I watched in stupor with a flannel in my mouth wondering how I was going to be able to talk to two hundred women waiting for me at Lytham St. Anne's town hall.

I have been lucky to have been invited by many Women's Institutes to the Fylde Coast to spend an evening with them, something I thoroughly enjoy and look forward to, from Booth's supermarket in Poulton-Le-Fylde, to the Norbeck Castle on the north seafront, to the Paradise Rooms at the pleasure beach, to the Winter Gardens Theatre, all well established and great venues that can transform themselves into anything required.

It has been over fifty years since I was first sent up to Blackpool to take charge of a Summer show at the then ABC Theatre sadly, no longer in existence, but then, the most prestigious venue for a host of big stars, also at the weekends to televise live shows, *Blackpool Nights Out* with both our own British stars but mixed with some of the best international names. More recently, it was turned into a lap dancing club seating two thousand men and a rather oversized pole in the centre, it had a short life, a folly which the council ended fairly abruptly as questions were being asked about the validity of such a venture and the respectability of the enterprise with its risky contents.

My emotions always play havoc with me when I return because memories of events and exhilarating times come flooding back. Although I have to acknowledge things have to change and go forward, I am still drawn to the good old days when the palace vibrated with wonderful shows, where families wanted to spend a whole week at the resort and could, due to the overwhelmingly entertaining and adventurous things they could get up to.

Now it seems, no-one wants to spend a week anywhere and the resorts are suffering. I can walk along the new promenade and see all the new creations and developments, but my senses yearn for the personality which gave the town the recognition it so deserved.

Over fifty years ago, my son was born at the Glenroyd Hospital in Blackpool, he became a sand baby. My show with Jimmy Tarbuck and Frank Ifield was just one small input into all the shows around.

Bruce Forsyth at the Winter Gardens, Danny La Rue at the Opera House, Morecambe and Wise on the North Pier. Matt Monro at the South Pier, Hylda Baker at the Queens Theatre and Al Read at the Grand Theatre and on it went, the season that everyone could enjoy.

And now, I feel a sense of loneliness when I walk around, the Circus in the Tower with no animals is perhaps a good thing but those animals, like those artists made the place come alive. For the children to see the elephants taken down to the sea was enthralling.

I suppose for me, I could not find a better environment for my talk for I am accepted on two fronts as I recount my life in the theatre and with the animals, I encounter an understanding from the women for life as it was. Their town is synonymous with beach donkeys and having been a bastion of light entertainment for so many years, what could be more fitting for me to step back into a story unfolding the two elements side by side, like slipping into a comfortable pair of slippers.

My talk at the Winter Gardens Theatre in front of the Federation's Annual Conference was something special that I have not forgotten. Over one thousand seven hundred women from all over Lancashire gathering to celebrate their year. It was a welcome homecoming that I hadn't experienced and to be truthful, not since. It was special, the donkeys were brought up from the beach and some of the posters of my old shows were put up on the two screens either side.

That night, for the first time, I ran out of books. I sat in the foyer afterwards amongst the women, we talked for hours sitting under the marvellous life size statue of Morecambe and Wise who I had the joy to work with over six years, we remembered, we rejoiced. We even recounted some of the things that meant so much to us all in different ways.

At Booths in Poulton-Le-Fylde, the WI took over the first-floor cafe in the evening and there were about fifty ladies having done their shopping downstairs heading for the talk upstairs. Because of my connections and work in the town, the talk became more like a question and answers session unlike what I was used to. A long reflection of not only a time passed by but also a hope, an insight into how any of us were going to get it back to where it was with a modern twist able to please all ages.

When *Strictly Came Dancing* at the Tower Ballroom for many, a past glory was reaffirmed but it was sadly drawn back to modern times as some of the dancers were set upon in local night clubs in the town centre after the show. But as a nation, we welcome and embrace such a vivid programme with all its colour excitement and joie de vivre so, that was the theme that encompassed the Poulton meeting, it became an interesting forum rather than a talk just from me. We talked together about things that mattered.

At Lytham St. Anne's, I was booked at the town hall on a Monday morning to address the WI. Annie and I love Lytham, we walk along the front and sit staring out at the estuary for perhaps longer than we should. We look forward to our meals in many of the quality restaurants or coffee in the cafes. Sadly, I fell again, this time on the pavement right outside the town hall. I fell flat on my face, hitting my chin with force on the concrete pavement, knocking out several more teeth, there were now few left. Passers-by were so kind. They helped Annie to find the teeth and put them in a glass of milk which again we wouldn't have thought of so that the dentist could decide.

What to do next? I knew what he could do next; that was to start work quickly on a nice set of new dentures but I still had a talk to do in an hour or so, after sitting in Gusto's restaurant outside with a warm flannel in my mouth for half an hour, I went in and did my best to look normal.

The women accepted there was something wrong, but they were too polite to ask, and I wasn't in the mood to tell them what had happened.

As I was apparently having trouble standing up these days, as it happened again six months later in Crosby down the coast a little on a lovely sunny Sunday, down I went again, same fall over yet another paving slab that hadn't been checked and was sticking out, this time the last of my good teeth were on the prom. Again, local passers-by came rushing to help. We stopped the bleeding, out came the cup of milk again for the dentists. The only worrying thing was the young lifeguard on duty couldn't help and really didn't have a clue what to do.

Fortunately, an off-duty paramedic stepped in valiantly and saved the day. A very sweet boy of around ten kept following me asking if he could buy me an ice cream as it would help, it renews your faith, doesn't it just? He was so sweet emphatically describing how the ice cream had helped him when he lost his teeth. It was such a kind gesture from one so young, I was able to drive home and have everything repaired for the next day's talk in Kirkham.

I relate all this to you because I hope you will understand when I was asked to go to the Low Wood Hotel in Windemere to stand in at short notice for a celebrity who couldn't make it. I was stunned to learn that I was sharing the evening with an eminent dental surgeon from one of the country's top hospitals. He used a video screen to show the work he was famous for, like routine root canal work and jaw reconstructions. Well, with my recent dental history, I decided not to watch and sat outside on a bench soaking in the lake and all its attributes. I had asked if I could go first but they refused my request insisting the ladies might like some light entertainment after their session with the surgeon. What I found quite amusing and revealing was that the surgeon had a wonderful sense of humour as he was describing scenes of utter carnage making my dental experiences inconsequential. Apparently, he presented the whole thing in an extraordinary way. I wish I had watched but one or two of the women did relate that some of the operations were hard to take even if he made light of them. I did alright in the end and even the surgeon enjoyed my little asides about my episodes of dental obliteration and the way he would have probably dealt with it.

Chapter 14

May

Kendal WI

For whom the bell tolls

When I was asked if I would attend the Cumbrian auditions in Kendall, I put to one side all my misgivings on the subject and agreed to go to their 'speakers finders' day mainly, I have to admit, because of my love of the district. I was not going to let any past difference get in my way of an excuse to walk and marvel at the Cumbrian scenery and if I had to talk to do so, then so be it.

The drive to Kendall was straightforward, taking just over two hours. We stopped at Kirby Lonsdale for lunch and walked around the lovely square and village which I remembered with much affection from my filming days when I worked on a rather sinister drama with the actor Donald Pleasance, an actor who specialised in sinister parts, yet when he removed the make-up and the costume and relaxed, was the sweetest and gentlest of men and great fun to be with.

Eventually, we found the hall at which the audition was being held. We carried our stuff in and were led to a waiting area. By this time, I was actually feeling unwell for some unknown reason, I had been coughing all the way up, so Annie went out to try and find a pharmacy for some linctus to get me through the talk.

In the waiting room, there were five other speakers preparing themselves. The first procedure was to receive the usual lecture regarding sticking to our allocated time of fifteen minutes. Should we go over the allocated time, we would be in serious contravention of requirements and suffer the ultimate penalty. We would apparently be given a warning three minutes before the required cessation, that would give us enough time to wind down and finish. Should we not take that instruction, the bell would toll at fifteen minutes and keep going to force us into submission.

I was rather anxious, the way the cough was going, that I would be unable to complete fifteen minutes and like a boxer under duress and on the canvas, the sound of the bell could well be my saviour. The other speakers took little notice of these important announcements or the instructions, it was just accepted like a member of a cabin crew explaining the fatal scenario should the aircraft crash and what should be done in that situation. Some of them had obviously been here before and it hadn't exactly changed their careers for the better, it seemed.

What did amaze me, as I made inroads to my impending illness with a large kitchen roll Annie had brought along to assist my needs, along with a ghastly tasting cough linctus which the chemist had assured her would clear anything from coughs to drains, was that I noticed that all the other five participants were not exactly speakers, they seemed more affiliated to variety and the cabaret circuit rather than the educational requirements held so dear by the Women's Institutes.

A rather portly gentleman removed a baby owl from a plastic container small enough to take a sandwich or a biscuit. He placed the owl on a make-shift piece of driftwood and the poor creature just attempted to balance and revive himself from what must have been a traumatic journey in such a confined space. Eventually, the bird came around and regained a modicum of strength required to just perch straight and shake himself down, removing the bits of sandwich he had actually had to share the plastic container with.

It was revealed that the owl was actually female and called Teddy, not the name I would have immediately associated with an owl. But she was a lovely little bird, soon spreading her tiny wings out with that wonderful stare owls have, then able to turn their heads completely around in a circle which I have always wished I could do, allowing you to see behind as well as in front. She didn't take her eyes off me for quite some time, of course, Annie had fallen madly in love and asked if she could handle her for a second or two which the handler agreed with.

After retrieving the bird from Annie who was reluctant to return it as she didn't want to see it replaced in the small sandwich box, the handler brought out something rather unseemly and placed it on the piece of driftwood which looked to me like a small rodent but Teddy wasn't keen and showed more intelligence by leaving it for later or perhaps never. It was looking now as even Teddy was looking forward to actually being put back in her sandwich box which I was beginning to sympathise with.

Another gentleman on the opposite side of the room was getting undressed and irrespective of a substantial female presence, sharing the confined space was getting completely undressed, if you get my drift, leaving very little to the imagination. He then climbed into what looked like a jester's outfit, one we would now associate with pantomime or medieval jousting. It was a very intricate affair with hundreds of buttons down the back which took him nearly fifteen minutes to do up. He got made up rather heavily, I thought, which I considered to myself might be a waste of time as the hall stage lightning was non-existent. In fact, there was not one light on the stage which might have blighted the effect he was trying to attain. He then got out a series of musical instruments I had never seen before in my life. A mandolin which looked at least three hundred years old and to be brutally honest, sounded like it when he tried, in vain, to tune it to his requirements which weren't apparent yet. It bore no resemblance to any recognisable instrument of any sort. I even tried, in kindness to him and the enormous amount of trouble he was taking, to take my mind back to the courts of Henry VIII but the sound just didn't match even those thoughts, it just resembled awful scratches. I was wondering how he was going to get a tune out of it, if that was the end product. A banjo was next but not the usual sort of banjo, this one just had two strings which he tuned to his liking but not to the baby owl's, who thought a friend was calling him from far off lands.

The owl was at least able to stick her head under her wings which is more than we could do under any circumstances. The last instrument was a zither. I had, in my time, auditioned many speciality acts for light entertainment shows both in the theatre and television but this one, I just could not fathom out, it was either going to be very clever or maybe extremely funny but I couldn't quite see how, as yet. However, I was eager to learn.

By now, my eyes were being affected by whatever this strain of flu was, I was even finding it difficult to focus as well as speak. Next to me, a young lady, attractive and dressed to kill in a tight evening dress was going through her scales. I had moved away, believing the last thing she required, apart from the bell, was my pending affliction and its illness. I imagined whatever it was that I was suffering from would not be of assistance or welcome and might impede her vocal renditions.

She brought out her backing tracks which she went through, putting them in the right order for her performance. I couldn't help wondering how she was going to get through the entire score of *Phantom of the Opera* and *Les Misérables* in fifteen minutes. She went through her warmup exercises, she obviously had a very pleasing voice and range, I was impressed and if she was going to be able to get through two rather long West End shows in the time allocated, I was *very* impressed. My worry was I had just seen the maritime bell, the lady had brought it out on the front row. It was so big; it could have been salvaged from the Titanic and probably with a comparative volume of sound when hit with her substantial mallet that she placed by the side of it.

The girl would never be able to be heard after fifteen minutes if this rather draconian woman was allowed to do her worst. Would she have to come back another month to perhaps complete this enchanting but lengthy session of musical greatest hits? She seemed undaunted by the prospect which gave me a certain confidence that the participants were determined to take the bell on as a challenge if nothing else. Looking through the door at the lady who was actually already holding the rope, even though the proceedings had not even started yet, there was no way she wasn't going to use it and assert her brief moment of glory on each individual attempting to get their life's work over to an unsuspecting audience in just fifteen minutes.

A gentleman then appeared from the toilet with less baggage than everybody else. He wore a multi-coloured coat, and baggy trousers. I noticed he had writings on the palm of both hands obviously to remember the gags he was going to tell. It's an old trick but I thought to myself if he can't remember fifteen minutes worth, what's he going to do when he has to do an hour or so which is often required? He cracked a few jokes in the waiting room which worried him as the response was not quite what he expected.

By this time, I was losing my hearing as well as all other bodily functions, so his jokes were going unnoticed on the whole, as I was trying to hide a raucous cough which the chemist's remedy had actually accentuated and made much worse as time went on. I thought I would try and make the comedian laugh a little as I said, it was better if they didn't laugh as he could get more jokes out. It was meant to be a joke, but he agreed with me and rubbed a couple of jokes off his hand.

The kitchen roll ran out eventually as the last entry came in to prepare. A contortionist lady who was representing the flying ambulance service, a charity I hold in great esteem, but I was having trouble imagining how she was going to put the two things together. It was of no worry as I would be gone before she got herself out of the suitcase that she had with her to start her act.

It came time for the presentation. Annie had requested, due to my ill health and its deterioration and obvious discomfort in actually now trying to stand up for five minutes, that it might be an idea if I could go first, that is, if the other participants didn't object. None did but she was told firmly that the running order had already been worked out and printed for the ladies and they would be totally confused by a change of order. So, I had to wait.

The owl was on first and immediately the handler apologised to the audience that he was not actually the person who normally travelled with the bird and that he was not conversant with the subject as this was the first ever talk in the matter. Good start

I thought. He explained rather sadly that his actual job at the aviary and bird sanctuary was to clean the birds out. I thought then with horror that that might be what he was actually going to talk about for the next fifteen minutes. Was he able, in fact, to fill that time on that subject which might have been interminable? The thought of him going on a little too long and the bell going off, my mind immediately worried for Teddy who might be so frightened she might leave the driftwood prematurely and fly away never to be seen again, but that might be good, I thought. The handler took a good option and suggested to the audience that if they wanted to come out to the foyer in the interval, they could meet the owl and he could answer all the questions then and there. A clever move, I thought but listening to his rendition, probably well advised. However, the lady at the front was angry that he had finished before his time as she had been aching to hammer her maritime piece of equipment relentlessly, determined that the large audience would understand she knew her job and position, that the sound would carry and the effect would be devastating if not adhered to, it seemed to her that it was obviously irresponsible to cart it all the way in if it was not going to get used.

The lady singer was cute, she seemed to be well known and recognised by a good part of the audience as she explained that she had entertained at most nursing homes and day care centres in the locality. Her renditions went down very well but the excerpts from *Les Misérables* lasted well over fifteen minutes and she still had *Phantom of the Opera* to complete. But it was clear from a member of the committee who had strategically moved close to the dreaded bell ringer that she was being warned off hammering it and not to use her authority just to allow this lady to finish in recognition of all her good works and volunteering for local organisations and the elderly in Cumbria. Quite right too. It gave me hope that in my present condition I might be given the same treatment, but it was unlikely as the woman would now be hell-bent for leather on using the bell on everybody else without exception.

The court jester I am afraid, did not go down well. The bell was an actual relief and got him out of trouble. His instruments were not appreciated, his choice of numbers rather obscure and difficult to comprehend but he seemed happy when he came off that he had actually lasted as long as he did. I assumed he must have had a similar reaction elsewhere. A shame but maybe he had done us all a favour in that the woman had so enjoyed her time on the bell and the joyously loud sound it had as she intended reverberated around the hall with deafening effect and that perhaps meant that now, she would be a little more lenient to the rest of us who were left to worry about it. Unlikely though.

The comic just scrapped his fifteen minutes, he was very careful not to overstep the mark, his football jokes didn't do the trick with an all-female audience and his rather risky innuendos proved a little unpopular as the audience got restless. After the comedian, it was announced there would be a tea break in the front of the hall for half an hour to refurbish their appetite for the second half and the last two participants.

I thought this was a risky move as I was unsure if I was going to last another thirty minutes. The illness was beginning to show rather worrying symptoms now, even my balance was not now insured as stable, so Annie and I took advantage of a hot beverage, hoping it might do the trick.

It didn't.

Initially, I struggled on to the stage and put my easel up, it was not hard to notice the woman at the front had renewed her grip on the bell so I was left in no quandary that she was going to use it if necessary and, had I not been so unwell, I would have fought her with everything I had but the will was not there and I fainted.

All very embarrassing but no bell. I recovered enough just to sign off and Annie helped me off. I apologised to Annie for dragging her all the way up country and not being able to achieve what we had come to do, but astonishingly whether from pity or kindness women did come forward to book the talk.

We travelled home slowly stopping off at the Kendal General Hospital where I was attended to and informed that I had a form of pneumonia which was giving me back and shoulder pains and respiratory problems. They advised me not to drive home but when I said I really wanted to, antibiotics were subscribed to enable us to get home.

The pneumonia went on for some weeks, the awful matter was that Annie went down with it too, so the two of us found it difficult to nurse each other.

We were also anxious in that we had a busy month ahead, it is no choice to let people down as the word spread as whatever the reason, it affects future work, so we had to find a remedy and quickly.

Annie and I completed four big WI meetings with pneumonia although it was hard. We both concluded that if you're really unwell, extremely ill or facing your maker, the safest place to be is in a WI. They seem to know what to do, certainly know what to say, the advice is always welcome on the spur of the moment, their remedies and recollection of how they themselves got through it are invaluable and fill one with hope and expectancy.

The pre-med talk from women who insist they have suffered from exactly the same thing and recovered whole heartedly is always encouraging, the ladies who informed me with a certain authority that their husbands had died of it, didn't have quite the same effect but the various diagnoses are always worth listening to and adhering to as some of it often goes right back to the land girls when antibiotics were not invented.

Chapter 15

June

Rainhill WI

Passion for Fury

Rainhill WI in Lancashire has a very special place in my heart. It started off in the usual way, hard to find, difficult access, a steeper than normal staircase to negotiate, no-one taking much attention on our arrival, just another speaker, another deep intake of anaesthetic, so no-one was that excited about what was in store tonight as yet.

On arrival into the hall, tables were being laid in order of importance and status, no visible suggestion of any further requirements or assistance other than the comfort and accessibility of those in high ranking positions. No clues as to where to install ourselves or our props until first, the room is made ready for the monthly assembly.

The four corner stone tables were out and decked, one for membership, one for a raffle, one for enrolment and one for tonight's competition which was small and empty due to the fact that the theme of tonight's talk had not given them sufficient information of its nature to gather a responsive amount of items to compete against each other.

There was an extra table for second hand books, flowers, the last table was decorated with a magnificent sampler, signed, it seemed, by hundreds of women, dedicated to the cause, an indication if one was needed, of forthcoming events and what the woman at this institute, clearly expected of their membership. The small but effective pot plant decrying the president, was in residence this evening.

I noticed from all this setting up and activity that this meeting was to be held in the round and that there were over a hundred seats set. So it would appear without having been informed, I would be speaking in the round with the audience surrounding me, something that I would have to consider carefully when laying out my visual aids so as everyone got a good view and were able to see everything appertaining to my performance.

One lady was crossing the floor with great difficulty lugging an enormous display board which was covered in photographs and notices. She came to a halt next to me both glad of the rest but also concerned that I was displaying complete anxiety as to where to set up and put out all our equipment. Although breathless, she could sympathise with my malaise about where to go or what to do next. She was obviously annoyed at having been given the task of heaving this heavy and enormous piece of furniture around and I was just another obstacle to overcome.

I announced bravely that I was tonight's speaker because so far, nobody had asked. This didn't go down too well, as the last one had, apparently, not knocked them off their feet with excitement or interest. She explained, in no uncertain terms, that the last talk had been underwhelming to say the least. She said she would find someone who could assist me explaining that she had no idea where the lady, whose job it was to welcome the speaker, was. As yet, she had not turned up as she had taken the wrap for booking the last one. With that, she took a big deep breath and hoisted the display board in an upright position and carried on pulling and panting across the floor.

A rather excitable woman made her way across the floor to us trying to avoid the dangerous looking display board, she meekly and unassumingly asked me if I was Mr Stirling, a question I was able to acknowledge with a certain confidence which seemed to put her at her ease. She seemed to be pleased that I had indeed arrived but started to show unease when I asked her if she could possibly indicate to me where I could set up. This seemed to be a responsibility she was not aware of, visibly not on her list of things to be done. A look of horror spread over her countenance as she saw Annie gliding over the floor with flight cases and easel. She asked me in a whisper, so as not to upset anyone close by, how much room was I going to require?

After answering her question by adding that I would require two trestle tables, I could see by her pale complexion that this was too much for her to take in or deliver without further consultation. She was going to need help to sort out this mammoth problem and request out. There seemed to be a look of utter disbelief on her face that I was now asking her to renegotiate the whole layout of the room which had taken the women hours to put together and only the St. John's ambulance lady in attendance that evening could now deal with her fragility.

Now the tea ladies arrived which transferred everybody's attention, the cakes were admired, the sandwiches, buns and light refreshments nearly got a round of applause on entrance. I am now to gather that this is to be the group's annual invitation to neighbouring clans to join together under one roof. They are expecting a hefty crowd. All the more reason, I thought, that I should now be getting a little more attention than I was actually receiving, especially if this meeting was, as I was being led to believe, to mean so much to them.

The president arrived to the usual fanfare of a well-rehearsed overture, welcome and admiration beset on her by the masses as she walked slowly around the room admiring but requesting in the same breath certain changes to the décor and seating so, as she put it, the setting was absolutely fair to all groups in attendance, brushing past me, she inspected her table to see all was there and accessible for the evening ahead.

It was at this point that she noticed Annie and I standing in the corner of the room trying to keep a lady on her feet who had nearly fainted on the request for two trestle tables. We must have had a vacant expression as the president inquired from her equerry who, in fact, we were.

She was obviously told it was tonight's speaker and his wife. She looked at her sheets of paper on her table for notification of who actually was speaking and what it was all about but the news had not as yet filtered through, so the lady who was now slowly recovering next to me was summoned across the floor to her table which she just managed but looked the worse for being picked for interrogation.

After a short discussion, where the shaken lady was advised to go to the kitchen and see if the ladies could make time to make her a cup of tea, the president herself made the journey across the floor in my direction. She introduced herself in the hope that I would do the same, which naturally, I complied with. She seemed keen that I gave her a clue as to what she might expect from me this evening, whether I thought the large crowd would be able to enjoy the contents and the presentation as their last speaker had not enthralled with a talk relating to his local garage and car maintenance.

I explained the talk was entitled *Toytown to Buckingham Pa*lace, the last part she understood but she was having trouble with the Toytown bit and as I never like giving away my trump card before I talk, I mentioned that I thought it would amuse her but by the reaction and the glare she gave me, I was not so sure it would have the desired effect, so I tried to evade her question which didn't lead to a good start.

The president informed me that she had received a request by the local ladies' rotary for tickets for tonight as guests. Apparently, I had talked there some months ago with some success. This I assumed, would endear her to me, lessen her anxiousness and overall despair from the last month's debacle but it didn't seem to go all the way to alleviate all concerns. She seemed to worry that if it wasn't any good, she would get it in the neck so there was no pleasing her. I would just have to do my best to win her over when the time.

I explained in detail what I required, as the lady next to her sank down on one knee, that I needed time to set up as the talk was going to be in the round, that I would be displaying some important visual effects on easels and I would need time to work it out properly. She told me in as much detail, that when she had finished her short address, she would allow time for me to set up. Would that be alright? We agreed quickly to be able to get on with it and to save the poor creature trembling next to me any more pain and suffering.

We agreed terms rather more balanced in her favour but workable for me, if they gave me the time.

The room being laid out in the round, I found quite interesting, reminiscent of my Royal Exchange Theatre times in Manchester when one had to perform in the round and to high galleries at the same time.

It was a good education because it taught us how important it was that everybody should be able to see everything from every vantage point. I was, I confess, looking forward to this challenge.

As the ladies from Rainhill arrived, I became even more excited about this evening's outcome, listening and studying them as they flowed in. I was gathering information and a prevalent sense of humour was coming across that I have always so admired.

The president took her meeting before my talk and her short address, as she had put it, finished just an hour after it started. However, I have to admit, it was the best address I have ever heard. She was informative when necessary. She had a good grip of her audience without being in anyway patronising. She dealt with matters with aplomb and a good deal of hefty and worthy belly laughs along the way. She seemed to know everybody by name which was impressive as there were over a hundred and fifty there. She had even researched the guests and got their names in her anecdotes, birthday greetings and matters of general importance were conveyed very amusingly with a very professional sense of entertainment, in fact, a little too amusing for my liking as I was having to follow her and she was not making it that easy.

Everyone stood for *Jerusalem*.

While the meeting was in progress, Annie had gone over to the bric-a-brac stall and bought all the paperbacks, a yellow scarf, an enormous plant that we were going to have trouble getting in the car afterwards, and a WI shopping bag with Rainhill WI emblazoned on it. I was both anxious that at this stage, we might not necessarily want to remember this night if it didn't go well and that the bag would be a reminder of a defeat, but Annie always seemed to know better and evaluate the night correctly. I was also anxious that our fee might not cover what she spent at the stall.

Rainhill ladies epitomised for me the North West and its natural assets, there was a very prominent Liverpool drawl mixed with a Mancunian tone. They were down to earth with strongly held values and beliefs for both each other and for their community. The strength comes across when you address them face on, you know immediately that they will not beat about the bush, if they don't like it or get bored, you will receive the news quick and fast and be under no illusions.

My time with Billy Fury always comes under intense scrutiny but especially in the North when I start to relate my time working and producing him, I do stop to let the grunts and groans from certain women subside, explaining to them why, being the nervous and anxious boy he was, that he was so frightened at appearing on stage in front of a frenzied mob. I relate that my job not only included looking after his professional side, but I also had to clear up the stage of half the women's lingerie from knickers to tissues, to even dresses and such like. As I am relating this in some detail, two women at Rainhill get to their feet and announce they how proud they were to have been able to go home practically naked after the show at Great Yarmouth but they were lucky because they came around the back and waited for Billy to come out of the stage door but he never did. He was so scared that he used to go out via the fire escapes or such unexpected doors so as not to be massacred. Both ladies were adamant they wanted to thank me. I couldn't think why but I was to learn that although they were bereft at not seeing their idol and getting their programme signed, apparently, I appeared at the stage door with all their clothes so they were able to go home at least with some of the clothes they came out with and save an intense family row.

Being with Billy was a revelation and when I bring up his image, it always gets the biggest reaction even from the younger audiences who were not around at that time. He was the most gentle and kindest person I ever worked with and we got on so well for two years. I always feel a sense of pride when the response to him is so positive.

I have never forgotten in Liverpool, a lady standing up and saying how much she enjoyed *Noddy in Toyland* at the Royal Court Theatre, Liverpool and that the following evening, her mother took her to see Cliff Richard at the theatre opposite, the Empire Theatre. Cliff had just had his first number one, *Living Doll* and the theatre was filled every night with screaming girls going quite berserk but she said her mother was surprised when they came out and stated quite seriously, 'Cliff still didn't get the same reception as when Noddy came on yesterday in that car." It warms the cockles of my heart.

The only other pop star I had the pleasure of producing was Scott Walker at Blackpool and at Poulton-Le-Fylde in Lancashire. I was recalling what a lovely voice he had when a lady stood up and said, "He nearly didn't appear that night when we carried him away in his mini" and they did, I remember even the Blackpool fire brigade couldn't lift it to get it back to the stage door but ten girls had carried it over two hundred metres with a terrified Scott inside and she was one of the two herculean fans. She looked all demure and the mother of three now.

We had a great night. I even did my Hylda Baker impression which is normally reserved for close friends in the confines of my own home being risky and not totally perfect but that night, it went down especially well.

So along came my Albert Modley poem and my Al Read sketch which are even more risky, but they loved it, even though I had been scared to death they wouldn't remember who the hell they were, but they all knew. Annie, however, was wise and brought me back down to earth after the talk and she apologised for advising me not to finish with George Formby as that, she thought, might well have killed the golden goose.

The ladies seemed to relish the nostalgia. All the old radio shows I had appeared in as a child actor were appreciated and fun to bring out of my cupboard. It took them back to the family sitting around the radio being the only form of family entertainment they had so enjoyed and to me, that was gratifying.

I enjoyed my evening as much as I hope they did. Annie confirmed reticently that I had done well breaking with tradition as she usually likes to keep me down a bit, fearing I get above myself with excitement. Although she was critical of my entrance into the risky untried and unrehearsed pieces, picking out members of the audience for participation, she agreed this time it had worked, but she implored me not to try it again. She reinforced her intuition that Rainhill had been a special place with a physical crowd, that I should definitely not try that again as it would in all probability not succeed.

We enjoyed the carrot cake and I was booked for the rotary dinner for a month ahead. A few weeks later, I noticed a lovely review which the ladies from Rainhill posted on the internet. Thanks ladies.

Chapter 16

June

Castleton WI

The heckler

A formal invitation came to me from Castleton Women's Institute in Derbyshire. It came in letter form, which was unusual, not the normal e-mail or phone inquiry, the president had felt it necessary to make me aware of a recurring problem that had to be explained before I signed the all-important confirmation form.

The president had felt it her duty, over the years, to warn the speakers of possible interruptions that might transpire during talks. She explained that many speakers in the past had been unable to sustain the battering of interruptions and surrendered before the end in total defeat. Many resolutions had been passed to attempt to stop the lady but when broached and asked to refrain, apparently she was worse, taking into consideration the length of service to the aforesaid WI and the vintage membership that stretched back many decades, it had been agreed to just accept and let it be. She went on to explain that she herself, had many unsavoury encounters revolving around decisions and motions of little consequence to the body of women overall but always seemingly of great importance to her at the time. The lady in question was apparently well respected in the community with many accolades and several very successful community projects under her belt, but the problem was firmly set in the fact that she was fearless and totally outspoken. The warning came like a Government Health Warning: Not to tackle her on any account because it would finish as it has done many times in anguish and sorrow for all concerned. Her postscript at the end was that she would quite understand, having read all this, if I wanted to cancel the said booking.

Foolishly, it came to me as a challenge. I was actually interested in this woman and her reputation; I went about believing in totally the wrong way that I wouldn't have the same problems as many others. Why I felt this way, I can't explain, only to say that it was extremely ill thought out and under researched. I believed, firstly, that my talk was suitably established as good and entertaining, therefore, there would be few places she could intervene. Secondly, I felt that I could now, after five years, handle the odd heckler, as I needed to, on previous volatile occasions. Thirdly, probably the most inadvertent folly was that I actually believed that I could give the recipient the same back as I got. None of these philosophies were going to turn out even nearly accurate. I accepted the president's kind offer of an invitation to their group meeting with a note saying I would be surprised if I was unable to handle the odd remark as I went along my business.

The message came back to me stating she was delighted I had taken up the gauntlet and she assured me that the women of Castleton would support me as best they could.

The Peak Assembly Hall at Castleton is set out on the outskirts of the village and designed in a horseshoe shape. The front door being laid back in the centre with two rooms, one on either side of an attractive hallway. The speaker is placed in the hallway as the rooms on either side have ample vision to focus their attention on him or her.

The president was waiting for me at the front door looking rather matronly, as if she was on official duty to welcome me and escort me around the wards for an inspection. It was a pleasant welcoming with smiles all round but, I did get the feeling I was being sized up as to whether I was going to be able to get through the evening unscathed. Nothing was mentioned, although the president did drop a hint that she was so glad I had come early, enabling me to get set up without any interference, by which I gathered she was meant the fearless one.

It was finally disclosed, and I was publicly informed, that the name of the heckler was Melanie and those foolish enough to abbreviate it to Mel were immediately chastised and put in their place.

We set up our table and props and a lovely mug of tea appeared for both of us with biscuits, an unusual habit, as most groups wait until after the talk before wasting time or money on the speakers' perks, just in case a quick exit is more favourable for the participant or in this unique situation, a confrontation with you know who.

Both rooms filled up quite quickly but without any signs of Melanie as I thought, but the president put me right on that, she was indeed in her seat and looking demure and calm, a well-rehearsed and choreographed piece of work which put those about to face her at their ease but did not fool any of the members of the institute who were only too well accustomed to what was about to unleash on an unsuspecting speaker.

She was pointed out to me. I was glad to see that she was not right at the front, but quite well back with her friend Agnes who, I was reliably informed, was only brought along each month to agree with everything that was said and to be expected to be in full support of every word, however difficult and disagreeable it got. What a horrid job I thought. In appearance, though a very ordinary visage, she would not have stood out in a crowd as I expected, perhaps that was the very reason she had to use a different method to be noticed.

Agnes on the other hand was completely transparent, the very essence of a yes lady, she even dressed like her counterpart, same scarf and skirt, a real double act without the laughs.

I started the talk with Noddy as usual, normally a winning start, but I felt an unease in the audience and worrying expression on some of the front row.

The first salvo came in for a direct hit.

"You're too big to be Noddy, a grown man of your age trying to explain a childhood fantasy, it's not right."

I was prepared but perhaps, not for such an unpleasant aside and so soon into the talk, I had hardly had time to put my first photo up on the easel. When the women saw the image on the screen, they reacted in the normal and expected way but when I got the costume out that I wore age eleven and asked the ladies to try and get me back into it, there was laughter all around with the exception of two seats. Avril had inadvertently smiled at the suggestion that I could, in fact, have attempted to get back into it but our friend was having nothing to do with this amusing interpretation.

"Stupid, that's all it is. Very stupid, I haven't come out for an exercise in childish misbehaviour. I do hope there's going to be something of interest in the next hour and not just this drivel."

Annie was now showing some signs of mild anger, but I carried on regardless and with the visual knowledge that the audience was willing me to. I talked about my early school days in Soho in the red light district and how difficult an *Ofsted* inspector would have found it to fill all the boxes in without some doubts and I described the front door of the school facing the stage door of the Windmill Theatre with the girls having a quick fag in the intervals.

"Disgusting."

"But true," I shouted, now wanting to take her on, perhaps one of the worst decisions of my theatrical life.

"If I wanted to hear about strip clubs, nude shows, and brothels, I wouldn't choose to spend an evening in my local WI," she shouted.

Now members of the audience seemed to wish to come to my aid.

"Why can't you behave? You always give us a bad reputation and we all have to bear the consequences, it's not fair." She looked over at her president who had not yet summoned enough courage to acknowledge or reprimand.

The lady continued but the voice got weaker the further she got into her speech.

"I am actually enjoying this talk very much so far and I find the amusement appealing and makes me forget the tenseness of the day I have had."

I smiled at her in thanks and admiration at her rather lonely stance on my behalf, but Annie was feeling braver and actually applauded the speech.

I thought it about time I tried to pacify the proceedings and ask the ladies if there was anyone who was taking offence or found my stories unethical or even too strong and the response was heart-warming to say the least but it was not accepted by a certain party.

"Typical, you all seem to relish a bit of smut or filth and it's not becoming of our organisation, he'll be talking about the *Calendar Girls* soon, I bet."

"I will," I answered, turning on her forcibly. "I always take great joy and comfort in recognising achievements of such magnitude and the fact that they have enabled so many sick people with their wonderful folly which hit the headlines and gave the institutes so much publicity and respect.

"Respect," she shouted, "Just taking all their clothes off and parading around at their age in the nude and you call that respect? You need seeing to, advocating such rubbish and mistaken morals."

The woman had hit one flaw in her confrontation: she had now insulted or criticised the organisation of which she was a member and the president now had to stand up and face the affront.

"We all have our own views and opinions on matters and at times, it does no harm to convey those feelings, but to ruin our evening and to make our talented speaker endure such hostility is not something we as a group can allow, therefore, I would suggest you take your leave this evening, purely so Mr Stirling can give us his interesting and amusing talk without any further interruptions."

The president now needed back-up and she got it, as all the women stood up and applauded her efforts and the fact that she had not embroiled herself in an antagonistic set-to with the women whose antics had, for years, made life uneasy for them.

They all stood for some time, as it seemed that the lady was not going to leave of her own free will. She looked and scowled at poor Avril who was, for once in her life, going to vote against her friend and opt for a freedom she had sought, for many years.

I finished my talk eventually uninterrupted and it was successful, not only for its content but for the fact that it had been responsible for sorting out a long-standing problem that no-one could get their head around or deal with.

The lady was allowed back the following month, but she behaved, I understand, and Avril sat with three friends on the other side of the room so, in the end, sometimes, it does no harm to stand your ground.

Chapter 17

June

Hinxworth WI

Favourite story

I have had the pleasure to be in the company of some wonderful women in my last five years touring the country, some have had a lot to impart with some astonishing lives and jobs of such importance which they often relate in such a modest way but which have enthralled me. Their courage and common sense never cease to amaze me. I rarely leave a venue without stories resounding in my ears and often have to write down some of the experiences not only to keep a record but also to print some extraordinary occurrences and life stories that need to be kept for posterity, which most of the women find matter of fact but which we find exhilarating and totally inspiring.

In Hinxworth, one such lady came to my attention and I got a response that completely floored both Annie and I that evening.

I was once again talking about Noddy and I bring out that costume that I wore in my early childhood on the West End stage sixty odd years ago. I ask the audience that if there are three healthy, strong and agile women willing to help me, we could try and get me back in to it in aid of one of their charities. I suggest the car park as the obvious place to try.

After the amusement of that short, somewhat mischievous antic, a lady stands up, assisted by her two callipers right in front of me.

"That's not the one I made you," she states.

I stared at her having absolutely no idea what she was talking about.

"The one I made you, not as flimsy as that one you have in your hand, that wouldn't have lasted you a night with all the antics you had to get up to."

I was still having trouble comprehending what the lady was on about.

"In fact, I made you two, so that one could be cleaned every two weeks."

There was a pause, I looked over at Annie hoping she was grasping what was going on.

Again, she came back, "The ladies could have got you into mine, it was stronger."

Now the audience were wondering what was going on.

I looked at her again and back at the audience as her friend then stood up and supported her.

"She made your Noddy costume for you when you were a child. She has often mentioned it over the years how she dressed Noddy."

The penny dropped and now I was able to show my disbelief.

"My god," I said, "You really did that?"

"Yes," she said, "and I even recognise you now, sixty years later."

"My costume, all those years ago," I kept repeating myself.

She went on to tell the audience what a good Noddy I had been and how Enid Blyton, who was no easy lady to please, had been so taken with my performance.

I carry a stool around on tour so that I can sit on it if I need to and this was one moment when I was glad I had it there. On this occasion, I needed it.

Annie cried, not only because of the woman but most of all, because of what she represented. She rushed over to her and hugged her tightly, whispering a big thank you.

It's something I will never forget.

Chapter 18

July

Thurston WI

Contacts

Annie and I had never been to Bury St. Edmunds in Suffolk and doing our normal research, we found that it would be definitely worth a visit. We arranged to leave at the crack of dawn to arrive in the town at ten o'clock in the morning, to give us a full day before our evening talk in Thurston on the outskirts of the town.

We were lucky in that the sun was shining, not a cloud in the sky as we set off around this historic market town. We first found a lovely little tearoom opposite the abbey to have our breakfast which was delightful, served on a pewter plate with pewter mugs for our tea, already a flavour on the surroundings were appearing.

As we were already outside the abbey, it seemed a good place for a sightseeing expedition, so we crossed the road and entered. It was still early, so there were not many visitors, just a few of the faithful that spend each morning worshipping and seeking grace and solitude which there was in abundance.

We ambled around slowly, reflecting on the enormity and splendour but also reading as much as we could on our journey.

Sections of parchment depicting the site of one of the most important medieval monasteries, a great deal to reflect on, the doomsday book and its important meaning and consequences. We spent at least an hour in the abbey and lit two candles for our two dogs which we had lost so recently and were missing horribly.

We walked through the abbey ruins and the Coronation Park grounds which were breath-taking.

From the abbey, we made our way down the medieval high street with its ornate architecture and attractive array of unusual shops. Annie bought a beautiful donkey's head, the likes of which, we had never seen before. It was made by a New Zealand lady who specialised in animal heads and there were some fantastic ones hanging all around the shop. To this day, we bring out the head at the talk and it never fails to be admired.

It would have been too easy spend everything we had, so we stopped in the Georgian square and treated ourselves to a lovely lunch in what was a very affluent restaurant. On perusing the menu, Annie (always the cautious one until it comes to shoes), had decided that it was far too expensive, but (always flashing it about with universal optimism that we will rebuild later), I was determined to make our market town journey special and, with a quick visit to

Britain's last remaining Regency Theatre, a literary haunt of both Shakespeare and Charles Dickens, we were reminded that we had our modest presentation to set up.

Thurston community centre was a large gymnasium-type hall with rope ladders tied to one side. It was the hall of many purposes but tonight, solely for the annual get together of seven Suffolk institutes all congregating under the banner, the Thedwastre Group. It was an evening where the seven WI's and their respective presidents of participating institutes introduced themselves and had to give an account of the highlights of their year's activities which included a huge variety of events, talks, fund raising, trips and visits.

With only an hour to go, the place was buzzing with at least thirty women rushing around laying out the auditorium with over one hundred and fifty seats and firmly placing their coats and bags on the ones considered the best view. The kitchen was at full throttle, urns boiling up, toasters ready for the tea cakes and crumpets, the tables were being placed in the wrong places but after much shouting, even a scream or two, were rectified and placed correctly.

Sarah Robinson made herself known to us, a lovely lady and charming, with her well scripted and rehearsed welcome to us both. A feeling of well organised chaos was pleasing to see.

"Have you had a lovely day?"

"We have, thank you. We have enjoyed the trip very much and learnt quite a lot in such a short period of time," I said, trying to look well educated and interesting.

"All the Thurston ladies have been looking forward to hearing you. They all seem so pleased that both of you are representing us on our very important night. It is important that we show ourselves off as the others are a little larger than us. We are deemed the underdogs at times, but they all agreed at the committee meeting that you would lead us to success."

I felt rather like Richard the Third leading his army into Bosworth Field but look what happened to him. "My horse, my horse, my kingdom for my horse," were his last words as he was torn to pieces on the battleground. The vision of me shouting, "My donkey, my donkey, my kingdom for my donkey," was perhaps a little far-fetched but was ringing in my ear.

The room filled quickly and the noise of one hundred and fifty women trying to be heard over each other was deafening.

I was proud of Annie, who had spent time and a great deal of effort in making our displays very professional and pleasing to the eye. She had also, in her spare time at home, finished a tutu for the London Ballet for *The Dying Swan* and she had brought it with her to show the ladies that she didn't only muck out donkeys for a living.

Annie's past career of forty years, leading her to become one of the most in-demand couturiers and designers is not expressed enough as her shyness and retreat from public recognition is not sought but, when you consider, that shows and series like *Sunday Night at the London Palladium*, *Stars in Their Eyes*, *The Good Old Days* and so many others, relied on her totally and single-handedly, to design and furnish the stars and dancers with the appropriate costumes or dress. She even made all Norman Wisdom's suits in the Mr Grimsdale films. She made Englebert Humperdinck's shirts and her favourite job of all and the friendship the pair achieved over the years, was Marti Caine, whose wardrobe she embellished.

The women of Thurston had read up about Annie on the laptops and I got huge satisfaction when so many of them wanted to know about her makes and the designs.

The gavel came down and the evening started.

Jerusalem to start, as always and a minute to settle.

The president addressed her flock and neighbouring officials and women, and it came about that the first instalment of the night was the seven individual presidents standing and relating their past twelve months and their achievements.

I have to admit that six of them were pretty good, they stuck to a reasonable time slot, they got their news and views across within their designated time, so the audience did not fidget or show any signs of unease. It was not a who's best or competition between the six of them but that was to come in the shape of the last president.

Number seven, as I will call her, was formidable. She rose from her throne at the back of the hall, walked slowly to the microphone at the front, radiating a solid and fearfully well produced air of grandeur with a stylish attire which could only have cost a fortune. She prepared for her oratory. The make-up was remarkable, not one hair out of place, even though she had walked through a windy car park to get in; it was like a brick, totally staying where it should, and going to stay there for the duration, that was for certain.

After pausing and slowly looking around the audience, she started.

"Thank you for inviting us. May I compliment you on the turn out and the efforts you have gone to make us all so welcome."

The voice was truly awe inspiring; it was reminiscent of listening to the Queen's Christmas message.

"We have had a moderately good year at our village with some good monthly meetings, and some rather entertaining and successful open days, at my home of course."

I noticed, out of the corner of my eye, one elderly lady in the front muttering, "Of course."

"January started our year with our favourite television gardener, whether it be a small garden with little room for flowers and such or whether it be like mine, large acreages of lawns and beds, stretching as far as the eye can see.

There was a distinct murmur in the hall.

"February and the delightful undergraduate from Cambridge, a friend of my son, who rowed for his University on two occasions from Putney to Mortlake, in the winning boat on both occasions, a very tall fair haired boy with shoulders like a wardrobe, made my ladies quite hot under the collar."

"March and the Queen's private secretary for many years, Sir Robin Janvrin, thrilled us with his presence and his most amusing anecdotes from the palace. He was so funny and stayed with me as a guest for the night, we went on discussing his work until we were too tired to carry on and the sherry ran out."

"April and the actress who won *MasterChef* gave us not only a talk but a display and cooked something up for us. She won the series and has opened two restaurants and written three bestselling recipe books, so the ladies were keen to get hold of those."

She smiled here but it was not reciprocated by the majority, but her own members were well rehearsed in a co-ordinated response, so she gets the support.

"May and the piece de resistance ladies, one of the leading men from the seriously successful series,

Poldark made a few knees tremble. There was a flutter of fans as many of the ladies had brought themselves for the competition. He was extremely handsome and arrived in costume ladies and told stories from when he had to learn to horse ride and swim, two things, he was incapable of doing before."

A voice in the audience well concealed for fear of vindication. "I bet he stayed the night with the sherry, eh?"

She was not put out by this aside and retorted, "Indeed he did!"

"July was Graham Walton and I wasn't sure about this one, being the father of the sextuplets if he was going to be interesting. In fact, his life was hysterical, he turned out to be very amusing indeed," she said with less conviction than her other guests, but which brought another aside from the audience, "The best of the bunch."

"Well yes," she confessed, "With all the bathroom antics, all the girls wanting to wash their hair at the same time, all taking their driving tests on the same day, it was different'.'

"Speaker of the year 2013," shouted another voice from the back.

"Indeed, indeed," she was now losing ground, it was time for the finale.

"Finally, the Baroness who intrigued us all with her life of grandeur, the way she has kept her stately home going all these years without the help of the National T, a dear friend."

She then turned to our display of furry donkeys and theatre memorabilia. She had a grin which made my hair turn up at the back of my neck and the chairman too now intervened thanking the lady for her extremely interesting year and participation.

She hadn't thought of finishing quite so early, so she walked back in style but to a rather polite, if not subdued response.

The president had picked up my fear and anxiety at having to follow that array of names and celebrities, so she gave a lovely introduction which I was very grateful for but still with the feeling that I must not let them down tonight whatsoever.

Noddy was an instant hit, they loved him so that it got me off the ground, but I was not flying yet.

My narrative of the Italia Conti Stage School, where I trained as a ten-year-old was going well; the fact that the actual building was in the red light district in Soho; that it was flanked on both sides by the infamous Raymond Revue Bar, twenty four hours of strippers; and more, on the other side of an Anne Summers shop where you could get all the gear if you could actually physically handle it. Three doors down and a brothel, well attended day and night and the front door of the school was directly facing the stage door of the Windmill Theatre and the girls would stand outside with very scanty towels in their breaks and 'it never closed' as the theatre's publicity stated. So, what would an *Ofsted* inspector make of that with his clipboard and boxes to tick? This got them, the laughter was such that I now laid it on with a trowel and well and truly got them going.

The actors and actresses were well received and well-remembered. I tried extra hard to make the behind-the-scenes stories as strong as the on-stage goings on.

The donkey stories were exceptional at breaking them down in laughter and a few cases, some tears.

Finishing with the Queen and our private audiences, I was reaching the finishing line, so I got my crop and tried to get over the line first.

I had probably not matched her astonishing list of celebrity speakers and she had great contacts which I was told later, she never spread around.

By the way, she never booked me for her village do.

I was so delighted that in her speech of thanks, the president made comment that it was proven it's not 'who you know' all the time but often 'what you know'. That got the biggest response of the evening, so I was to gather by that that I had done my job and I hadn't let them down.

A lovely e-mail came through the next day from Sarah Robinson thanking Annie and me (see the appendices at the back of the book).

At the end of my talk at Thurston, I will never forget the young lady who presented me with a beautiful crown, made in a cardinal red velvet material with an ermine trimming and all around the sides replacing jewels where small miniatures picture all of the people I had worked with over my lifetime including Noddy and Muffin the Mule.

It must have taken her weeks and hours of meticulous work to do that for Annie and I and it really does look like the royal jewels. It travels with us all over the country and stands proud every evening on our production table for everyone to see and we always take note how thoughtful, clever and talented, the young of today are.

You know we love you and god bless.

Chapter 19

August

Euxton WI

Chorley's Angels

Four years have passed since our short excursion to Cyprus. Memories evaporate as time marches on but there are certain aspects of the working holiday and the island itself that we cannot erase. They are maintained at a high level by our three family members who are with us constantly and have their three baskets in the lounge, the bedroom and the office. They are our constant companions; they monitor every situation. Every visitor is looked after and the interest of the children who stay with us or just visit. Plus, of course there are our two handsome donkeys, so Cyprus stays in mind day in, day out.

At the start of a new week, Mondays are always hard to get into. Unlike most people, our Sundays are always hectic, so there is no rest, but we do take it easier on the first day of the week. We are not open to the public. We don't have children on day visit, just the ones who are actually staying with us. So, I was curious, when I noticed coming up our mile and a quarter long drive, a vision of four women laden with bags trudging towards the farm. It's quite a substantial hike of nearly two miles to walk, not many attempt it, as we are situated in a very rural isolated part of the National Park with no trains, buses or any means other than car to get us out so four characters to be walking towards us must only mean that they had a tough journey or rather a pilgrimage to get to us. I was hoping two things, firstly, that they had not got the wrong place and were not hopelessly lost and secondly, that they were not Jehovah's Witnesses who have tried many times to force their beliefs on us who also have been quite difficult to get rid of but I have always been ably assisted in that matter by my three Cypriot residents.

As the women got nearer, they came into my focus. They were showing signs of fatigue. I still had insufficient lens to instil any recognition, so I changed to my driving glasses and immediately homed in on the leader of the quartet. She had the stick and when she saw me, she waved frantically, almost collapsing into the grass verge but steadied herself and thankfully remained upright. The second woman had stopped, was leaning against a dry-stone wall panting rather heavily and drinking from her water bottle. The third seemed, from a distance to have lost all sense and equilibrium, the heat was getting to her. The last one had lost the will to live and was beginning to relieve herself of all her clothing bit by bit until she reached an acceptable temperature, this I had to counteract immediately, as the drive is not only for my use. Mornings and afternoons are very busy with the neighbouring farmers driving their tractors and other machinery up and down to all the fields which surround us. They are not averse, from time to time, to shout at the public to get out of their way and, a middle aged woman stripping to the bone in the Easter sunlight, would be far too much for them to accept without commenting out loud as they passed pulling four tons of cow muck. The comments could be misconstrued in many ways, some of which would, without doubt, be offensive, going for a quick laugh at the poor women's distress, something I was not prepared to tolerate. I was fairly sure she would be taken by surprise by the language and possibly the innuendo, so I had to nip it in the bud and suggest certain garments should be kept on, for now.

I was near enough to recognise the group as the infamous Chorley's Angels, the feline dinner ladies from our hotel in Cyprus. It was good to see them again. I lead them into the farm, it was a happy reunion, Annie immediately opened the conservatory, featuring her sublimely delicious cordon bleu tearoom and installed them in four comfortable wicker chairs, drawing the blinds to give them some shade from the sun. After a reunion and distribution of photographs of the cats, Annie suggested they rest as she would get their afternoon tea, this seemed to go down well with everybody.

Annie's afternoon teas are without any doubt the talk of Derbyshire, they have been for some time.

The ladies were not expecting what was about to be produced for them to devour. The three-tiered plate dish was the first thing to give the game away leaving no-one in any doubt that something special was about to happen. I could see Annie's deliberate attention to detail, her stand for quality as this was the Women's Institute, their reputation for cakes, jam and tea went before them, so she had to reach the mark. A selection of thinly cut finger sandwiches from cheese and tomato to salmon with cream cheese, Coronation chicken with mayonnaise and ham on the bottom rung, plain scones the size of a small loaf with clotted cream and jam on the top rung and a moderately huge portion of Victoria sponge with runny cream, all this supported with earl grey, mint or Twining's breakfast tea.

The women didn't let her down and as they had walked a long way. They were ready and the quality made the quantity unknown disappear fast, all was finished to the last crumb. As the ladies relaxed and where ready for a short siesta to let it all go down. I arrived to show them something that they would love to see. So reluctantly, they tried to lift themselves out of the comfortable chairs and follow me to the paddock close by and there, in front of them, stood two massive and totally handsome shining donkeys.

"Now girls, do you recognise these men?"

They showed little signs of recognition.

"Right, this is Sky and this Pathos." I looked at them, "Ring a bell?"

The women immediately got very excited and made moves forward towards them.

"Be careful, they are big boys and although extremely affectionate, very strong and very big, even we maintain a certain caution with them."

"They were so tiny last time we saw them being loaded into their crate that the British army had constructed for their journey to Manchester, now look at them."

"Beautiful," the other two commented, "They certainly fell on their feet."

At that moment as if on cue, Nico, Summer and Darcy ran out into the courtyard and everybody went into party mode. The rest of the day was just mayhem. And to finish it all off for them, I got Sky ready in all of his harness', got the donkey cart out of the barn and I drove the four of them back to Buxton and their train, an experience they said they would never forget.

A year later, the invitation came through, asking me to talk at one of their group meetings in Chorley at the Euxton Women's Institute, I accepted with pleasure but stopped short of taking Sky and Pathos which they requested, as explained, it was a little too risky. I didn't feel Chorley was ready for such an experience.

The day of the talk came around. We set off early to Chorley. The weather was not good, by the time we got on the motorway, we were battling through a monsoon which we had never experienced in our lifetime. On the radio, it was reported that the Whalley Bridge dam was about burst which would mean many villages would be under water.

My window wipers couldn't go fast enough to make things ahead visible; many vehicles had pulled into the hard shoulders unable to continue. The spray from lorries was not helping but eventually, slowly and with great caution, we reached the turn off and followed the road to the Methodist church hall where the group met each month.

We parked in the church grounds and sat for a while in disbelief at the power of the rain. Apparently, the one o'clock news stipulated that we had a month's rain in five hours and the damage was extensive around the country.

"There's going to be nobody here."

Annie agreed but, at that moment, a door of the Methodist church flung open and standing before us was an image reminiscent of paintings I have seen of the Archangel Gabriel.

The figure was a lady, though with an apron on and a tea towel across both shoulders, she was beaconing us in. We both made a dash for the door and got a months' worth of rain dropped on us. It was only a few feet and we were drenched.

"I'll make you some tea," she said.

"Is this where the group meets?" I asked.

"Usually," she said, "But the rain has been so devastating that they have had to go across the road to the Catholic church hall. So just get dry and it will probably stop soon."

Sadly, that was not the case, it just kept falling.

"There will be no-one here?" I said hopefully, meaning we could go home.

"Oh, they will be here, don't you worry."

We had our tea, shared the contents of her biscuit jar and made our way the three hundred yards across the main road and into the Catholic church car park which wasn't much different than the Methodist one, perhaps only in size.

Unfortunately, all the members of the institute turned up at the original and permanent hall which they had accepted for decades as theirs, only to be told that they would have to weather the storm which was now at tropical strength and cross the road to the Catholic enclave. To my surprise, they managed to do it and the vision of these poor women struggling in, absolutely destroyed, destitute and soaked beyond belief, was a sorry sight.

There were eighty of them that braved the talk and after a quickly constructed soup kitchen, the local hairdressers donating many towels for a good rub down, the talk went ahead.

At the end, the president was charming, she made a lovely thank you speech and the women seemed happy to have been washed away. What a lovely group they were.

Chapter 20

September

Calderdale WI

My favourite aunt

A short while ago, I was totally enthralled by a television drama series relating to the life of Anne Lister who emanated from Halifax in Yorkshire. I was intrigued because Annie and I had recently been to visit Shibden Hall, her estate and country home nestled high above her hometown. I was bowled over by the authenticity of the whole compound and the work that had gone into the entire project by the Calderdale Council. We had been invited to tour the house by members of the Halifax WI, as I was to talk in neighbouring Skipton that evening to one of their group meetings in aid of the Petal Children's Cancer Charity. I found Shibden Hall the most profound and moving epitaph to such a wide ranging and astute lady who had done so much for her town and had also had to battle through unequalled prejudices and hard times accorded to her for her sexual preference.

The hall itself is outstanding, relevant and pertinent to her epoch, untouched giving an immediate sensation of entering the period it depicts, portraying how difficult it must have been to stay alive, let alone live a life of one's own choice. The success of the excellent series and the award-winning performances had helped so much identify us with the enormity of what was considered such a crime in its time.

In the company of the Women's Institute, I believed there might be some signs of distaste of the life lead within these four walls. It was austere and very confined in space. The bedrooms were very small and inconspicuous, it seemed it would have been practically impossible for Lister to have concealed a good deal of what went on in the twilight hours. It was, at the same time, such an interesting house. The changes she herself imposed on sections of the interior were outstanding and very beautiful, perhaps a little over-indulgent but so clever architecturally, with such vision for her time in occupation.

One of the ladies was well conversed with the subject in front of us and managed to explain everything masterfully, in great detail, with much sympathy, in a way which covered the whole spectrum of the deception that had to be endured but without making it sound wrong in any way. Her focus was on the genuine feelings Lister had for the opposite sex, the way she dealt with it forcefully but with honest passion, undeniably not affecting anyone other than perhaps, endangering the reputation and lifestyles of the partners she chose as the revelations often became publicly known and sometimes lead to somewhat dangerous consequences. But the narration gave great credit to the mammoth work that Anne completed for her town of Halifax, so many ventures would not have succeeded or flourished without her intervention, input and ingenuity. There was, in this WI lady's view, a very important balance to make and to justify.

I listened carefully to the woman's clever narration hoping I could be as interesting and as entertaining to her group that evening. It was of huge benefit meeting with these ladies, giving me the insight and feeling they had for the enterprise we were witnessing together in this wonderful vista of commemoration to an extremely clever and observant landowner and entrepreneur.

I hope I am not stepping out of turn when I say that I felt an enormous sense of pride in this piece of natural heritage. Ann Lister has done so much for the environment and her much loved Halifax, nothing seemed more important to her, so to be judged at the end by her sexual orientation and not by her vivid accomplishments that benefited so many seems to me at the very least, unfair. What happened behind closed doors was not intended for public consumption, it would seem to me.

I had my own reasons to agree, as I was reminded affectionately of my favourite aunt Monica and my early life, and the short time I was able to spend with her in Paris where she lived.

Monica Stirling was a bestselling novelist and after the war, had come to prominence with her first autobiography, *The Pride of Lions*, the life of Napoleon's mother which was a great success. Apart from many novels, she also wrote autobiographies on Visconti and *The Wild Swan*, the life of Hans Christian Anderson which won her many awards. Monica was tall, attractive and elegant with a vivacious sense of humour covered with a shyness that focused attention on her vulnerability.

After the war, my mother was contracted to make a film with James Mason, *Candlelight in Algeria*. She had been very careful and cautious to give birth to me in complete secrecy in a small private clinic in Hampstead due to the fact J. Arthur Rank, her film company, did not credit publicly their leading ladies or starlets with any husbands, children or such baggage. They wished at all times to pull a veil over such matters insisting that the actresses in question keep their private lives completely under wraps, so as not to confuse or irritate the public who had been convinced of their free spirit and availability. Their motive being was that what you saw on the screen, you got in real life and that their status as romantic, available, leading ladies, remained intact.

My mother was finding it difficult to keep me isolated from the public and her employers which became a problem for her not wanting to relinquish the success she was achieving on the screen. I was quite a lively character even at a few months old. I had been given a great pair of lungs and I didn't act to orders or requests as required so, having me in dressing rooms or film location vans was out of the question.

My father was unable to help, having just been released from Colditz Castle, after three and a half years' incarceration. He had been fortunate to get a part in the film *The Cruel Sea* with Jack Hawkins and co, so his hands were also tied. He opted to hang on to a dingy in the Atlantic, cleverly reconstructed in Ealing studios but just as cold as the real thing, he used to say. So, my mother made advances to my aunt Monica, her eldest sister, to help her out and take me on for a few months while the work was finished. Monica reluctantly agreed after being pummelled by her younger sister with onslaughts like, "Surely you can help me just this once? We are family, after all," and the worse one of all, "I have, after all, got your mother living with me." Monica gave in under such pressure and I was sent to Paris to stay.

Monica lived in the centre of Paris with her publisher, she herself, was well known and mixed in high Parisian circles, in the company of Noel Coward and such dignitaries. On a personal basis, she was also well known for having preferences similar to those of Anne Lister and had made enormous inroads to have the whole situation accepted by all around her, so her circle of specially selected admirers and friends were baffled when she kept appearing in public with a baby.

I confess I was not an easy child; I was not happy in Paris with nannies and governesses that I couldn't understand who had been brought in to alleviate the strain and time on Monica's busy schedules. I used to show my anger a good deal of the time and Monica's partner had not endeared herself to me not being used to or even fractionally interested with the predicament Monica had found herself in. She displayed a certain disdain at having to have a child in her house. She also believed it was cramping their style with friends staying away from this domestic chaos which didn't bare well with their much-loved hospitality and party gathering which had been put to one side for the moment. Monica's partner was fairly fearsome which didn't help, Monica's close friends had always come to accept which one of the two was the feminine one.

The culmination of this unhappy episode was that I was sent home early as soon as my father was finally removed from the ice-cold tank and sent home with a slipped disc which meant corset and plenty of lying down. So, as he was housebound, he now had the job and unenviable task of looking after me.

A few years later, Monica and I built a very healthy and long lasting and loving relationship. Although I will never be able to write like she did, the fact that I actually wanted to, is very much down to her encouragement and enthusiasm. She was so happy when I had my first plays accepted and produced.

My sadness to relate is that at the end of the war, Monica was asked to accompany the American GI's into liberating the two most appalling concentration camps, Auschwitz and Buchenwald, the scenes she faced and had to write about and report on for *Life* magazine and the *Atlantic Post* were devastating, the horror was more than she could bare and accept. After a long struggle with years of depression, she took her own life in a hotel in Lausanne, unable to concede to the horror and inhumanity of what she had witnessed years before.

So it was that my thoughts were with her while I walked around Shibden Hall listening intently to the lady's narration, her careful and very respectful account of Anne Lister's life and works. Although Monica never had to suffer any of the disadvantages Lister had to endure, even after the war, life was not cut and dry for women living together under the gaze of publicity.

My talk that evening was at the Rendezvous Hotel in Skipton, it was a combined night that the WI were attending along with the White Rose Ladies of Yorkshire which was to raise money and funds for children with cancer and their need of the research for special drugs and ultimately cures.

I was determined to include in my talk that night, a short section of what I had seen and experienced during my day in Halifax, attempt to give an honest appraisal of our visit to Shibden Hall and how it had affected me. I was determined after all these years to pay homage to Monica with true and genuine love and affection and attempt to show what a valued member of our family and society in general she had been with all her wonderful novels and articles, even her war records which I have kept very safe all these years.

The women seemed pleased that I had broached the subject of our adventure together, the audience as a whole, were very kind in their response and seemed interested in both Monica's life and works as well and quite naturally, able to acknowledge one of the most wonderful Yorkshire women of the last century. I was thrilled to learn later that several copies of *The Pride of Lions* had also been ordered online.

My aunt loved children. She was also a great animal lover with cats scattered all over her flat in Paris. She taught children at certain colleges and schools in the art of writing. She had some notable successes with some youngsters going on to write and publish their own works.

As far as the WI members that evening were concerned, they seemed pleased that I had gone off track for a short while and explained my aunt's life and works. They were also pleased that I hadn't gone into any sort of criticism or ideology or shown any preference for any way of life.

As we both agreed, it is a very personal choice; way of life not to be criticised or judged as it was in Annie Lister's day, the only challenge being reserved for those who feel an obligation to do so and gain our respect in such matters.

I loved my aunt for being a wonderful woman. She showered affection on both men and women, she had equal amounts of friends of both genders and felt the same about them. The memory should be the person, the talent, the life and left at that.

I have never discussed this at any other talk, although I always open with the anecdote of when I was sent to Paris as a baby what a devastating effect it had on certain people. I know Monica would laugh and enjoy that episode as the anecdote is always enjoyed and understood by my audiences.

Chapter 21

September

Downham Market WI

The icon

We came off the M6 motorway at the sign for Clitheroe, down the slip road to the Tickle Trout restaurant and around the roundabout towards the Ribble Valley, very much a favourite haunt of ours on our travels around the country.

We passed the BAE Systems factory with the two impressive jet aircraft in their entrance prominently for all to see from the road.

A canvas of blue sky, not a cloud in the sky and even though our satnav was registering a temperature of minus one, nothing impaired the delightful Lancashire countryside.

The Ribble Valley then takes over with its formidable Pendle Hill, which seems to stretch on high, dominating forever. I have never been quite able to comprehend my wife's total fascination for the monumental and historical mound of earth which reaches for the sky. She never takes her eyes off it as we travel some miles and seems riveted by the tales of the Pendle witches and all that went on in the hills and its environment. She has read up on the women who were burnt at the stake and tortured by the local inhabitants for their supposed sorcery and witchcraft for which many were misunderstood and falsely accused as far, that is, as Annie is concerned. I can often be surprised at what grabs Annie's interest but the unfairness of matters past, do seem to register from time to time.

I was keen to go to Grassington on our journey as I was appearing in the Grassington festival in a few months and I had never heard of it but was reliably informed, it was one of Yorkshire's jewels and a fortnight celebration of some importance in the Yorkshire calendar.

We drove into the centre of the village which was a cobbled courtyard of beauty, quaint shops in a horseshoe shape and all exhibiting merchandise you would not find anywhere else: to call it picturesque would be an understatement. We meandered up the narrow lanes until we came upon the Octagon Theatre at the very top of the village. Intimate and charming, it was open, so we had a look inside to find an excellent form of lecture hall come theatre, seating a hundred and fifty in a circular shape. The front row being directly on the stage itself for intimacy.

The Octagon was beautifully equipped with a modern gantry of lights, a good sound system and various ingenious ways of closing it down or if needed, opening it up to suite the various artistic requirements. Annie was pleased to see that there were publicity posters for the forthcoming festival, and I was included amongst the better known which she felt showed a fairness that the lesser mortals had received the same treatment as the celebrities.

We chose amongst a variety of boutique coffee shops and cafes the Badger Tea Rooms in the courtyard, it appealed to us for its menu of typically Yorkshire delights in opposition to the latte and cheesecake in the other windows, although I am quite sure they were delicious too, but the Yorkshire toad-in-the-hole and Annie's Yorkshire omelette with local sausages and home grown accessories was a delight.

I had only one important observation that there was an expensive shoe shop in the courtyard, and I was making plans to get Annie past it without the use of our card. Annie can't pass shoe shops and shopping jaunts can be a nightmare but instead, she went into the bookshop next to the Badger Tea Rooms and brought yet another book on the witches.

We left Grassington and headed to Crago as I was keen to see the WI hall where the *Calendar Girls* started their successful crusade for cancer research, and which emanated in many actress' having years of work appearing in the West End and provincial theatre. I was keen to see the settings in the film but as is often the case, it was filmed in many villages close by to get the most attractive locations. There are plenty to choose from but sadly, we didn't have the time to find them. However, we did finish up in

Bursell which was a splendid backdrop for some of the film.

We reached Chatburn and our first sign to Downham itself, our destination for tonight's talk. Two miles further, there was the imposing and beautiful little village itself.

Driving down past the village church which dominates the whole scene with its small village green and seemingly very busy pub-come-restaurant on the opposite side, you are faced with a steep descent into what can only be described as heaven, you make your way cautiously through a row of immaculately kept cottages which have obviously had strict planning orders to be preserved and to remain as they were many years ago. All the small windows have wooden windows and shutters, the doors are all painted the same colours and the small but effective front gardens have identical dry-stone walls. There are no shops as such, but I noticed a school which fitted in to the architectural prowess of this out-of-the-ordinary beauty spot. We had to stop and just sit by the brook which runs through the centre with a picturesque bridge just about capable of taking cars but no heavy vehicles: even tractor and farm vehicles have a long round trip to get home.

After an hour break which gave as much pleasure as a week in Malta, we brushed ourselves down and made a move to find the village hall. There was, of course, no postcode, it was prominently advertised on the village notice board. My talk was festooned on the board but with the simple fact that the talk started at seven-thirty at the village hall. There were no clues as to where we could find the venue and after asking a teacher from the school, she assured us that if we drove up the hill in the opposite direction to the church, we would come across the hall on the left, great. We climbed the steep hill which was nearly a mile long until we reached the top and then continued on an equally steep descent which went on for another mile with no visible sign of any openings or properties, I turned the car around and drove back. As I was just going over the brow of the hill, Annie screamed at me to stop, at which point, I was fearful that I had run over a pheasant or even a rabbit or some other four legged inhabitant but it was fortunately not to be. Annie had found a vital clue in the shape of the council's wheelie bin with the initials WI emblazoned all over it, a few yards ahead, concealed by foliage, in case somebody actually found its whereabouts, was a vast car park with the hall at the end.

Women's Institute halls have been designed and built to melt away into their surroundings in an ingenious way. The camouflage is always masterful, one feels that only Capability Brown could have designed or done justice to such bastions of secrecy, planting trees carefully and surreptitiously to hide certain landmarks and visual assets which give the whole game away to the naked eye. This village hall certainly looked impregnable with more fortifications than the local castle which itself was quite impressive. The only mistake in the whole conception was to leave the dustbin outside the gate. That would have been a huge disappointment to Capability Brown but full marks to Annie for spotting it. One would have expected bushes, hedge leaves and twigs to make it blend into the landscape but obviously, the one lady responsible for it had made a drastic mistake which might cause damage to her duty as the member responsible for refuse collection.

The ivy was all over the walls with the front door just visible but locked at present, so we sat in the car waiting for someone to officiate and it wasn't long before that trusty little red Fiat 500 came hurtling through the gate at formula one speed, kicking up stone and aggregate all over the place, leaving a trail of dust behind it. It screeched to a halt by our side.

An attractive middle-aged woman got out unaware that she had showered us in dust the equivalent of the Sahara Desert and marched over to us, introduced herself and asked if we needed any help to carry our stuff in which we declined and noticed when she opened her boot, that she had twice as much as us.

The main bulk of the women were not far behind now, driving in and settling in the hall. While we were setting up, I was encouraged by the sense of humour of three ladies, obviously the very best of friends, imparting jokes and gossip to each other in a hugely amusing manner. They were laughing but they were also making us laugh in doing so, they were simply fun with a delightful Lancashire brogue. The three of them were at times in hysterics at every sentence which was so refreshing it made me feel at home like the old days when pros got together before the shows started and made up stories of how the days had been.

As I hoped, the talk went well, and the three women could take a good deal of the credit for their participation and laughter. They heckled me in a wonderful way and always in a manner which everybody could enjoy. They were responsible in many ways in making their ladies appreciate my stories.

I loved my evening but then came the bombshell.

I had spent the whole day racking my brain as to why I felt as I did about the village itself. There's always one moment in one's life when we experience a sensation which gives you a real jolt. For a moment, you see something that you have either dreamt about or had a premonition about. For a second or two, it's very scary. You see a setting that you have been in before, you even speak to someone that you have spoken to before but only in thought, not in reality. Something appears for a very short time which just knocks you off your feet. It happened twice to me that very day. I had been there before, although I knew, not in my lifetime. I had spoken to people. I had even conversed with the three women in times gone by. I kept all these thoughts to myself in case someone suggested a rehab institution or something, but the answer for my dilemma appeared in front of me at the end of my talk.

The president came over to me behind my table and thanked me. I was fondly receptive because she had given me one of the nicest thank you speeches on behalf of the ladies and I was moved.

"You look tired, Mr Stirling. Are you going to be alright driving home?"

"Yes, thank you," I said.

"I am just puzzled by a feeling I have had," and I explained my moment of unexplained visions.

"You're not the first."

"Really?" I hoped she would elaborate.

"Yes, and especially you and your life and stories."

"How come?"

"Well Downham was the setting for the film *Whistle Down the Wind*. Many feel something when they come here but aren't aware of that fact, that they have experienced its presence on film, plus the fact that it became a cult and a classic. We have lived off it here all those years."

I was truly taken aback as everything now fell into place there and then. The penny dropped, as it were. "Well, how extraordinary,' I was really taken aback.

"There's something else that I don't tell everybody but naturally all the villagers know, but I was cast by Richard Attenborough to play Hayley Mills' young sister in the film which was directed by Brian Forbes."

I just stared at her incredulously. "You're joking." Those words just came out. I hadn't thought about it and the response wasn't worthy of what she had dropped on my lap. "You're an icon."

"Not quite," she muttered. "I never did another part afterwards, even though Brian Forbes tried hard to change my mind as he thought I was a natural. The thing he used to say to critics and members of the public was that he never once had to actually direct the children, not once, and some of it was not scripted. We were just told what to say and then just said it."

I was taking my time taking all this in.

"Didn't you want to do another film?"

"Not really. Had it not been dark, John, I would have taken you around the village and shown you all the locations. Please come back and see us again and we will do it."

I thanked her profusely, commenting that I felt it a shame she hadn't stayed with it.

"My parents' farm needed the next generation to survive, I also felt very strongly when a child makes huge impact on the screen, it does not always lead to other things, but certainly did for dear Hayley, she was wonderful, so helpful. Let's face it John, I had some lovely scenes and moments with Alan Bates in my own barn. Who can say that?" she laughed.

I was close to Hayley Mills and her family as my mother had acted with John Mills on many occasions in film and theatre. My aunt had built Muffin the Mule which Annette Mills, Sir John's sister, accompanied on the piano for many years, so I was keen to meet up and have a meal together in London.

We met at the Grosvenor House Hotel in London as Hayley was filming in the city for a new television series.

"So, you've talked in Downham, have you?" she asked.

"Yes, and I loved every minute," I replied, and I went on to explain to her how surprised I was, "When Christine told me she had been part of the film with you."

"Yes, and a very big part, both the children were brilliant. Without them, things would have been very different, it could have just turned out a little B picture of little importance. The small Yorkshire boy stole the film and the little girl was right on the button: she was great."

"She's now the president of the Downham Women's Institute, she did tell me why against being asked, she didn't want to go on doing it."

"Yes, everybody wanted to sign the two of them up, the boy went on for a short while to do things but Christine was quite adamant that she was going to stay at home and be a part of the family business at a very young age and everybody accepted that. But it was a shame."

I said jokingly, "It never did you any harm."

"No," she said, 'But, between you and I, there have been times when a life on the farm would have been nice and very enviable, maybe I would have had a crack at being the president of the Downham Women's Institute, who knows?"

Chapter 22

October

Inglestone WI

Throwaway props

We arrived early at Inglestone parish hall due to having talked at a U3A morning meeting at Bury St. Edmunds. The journey across the country had not taken as long as we expected, so we had four hours to kill in the small Essex town.

We walked up and down the high street, glancing in the windows of mostly charity shops from cancer research to animal welfare with only half a dozen other outlets and seven cafes. We chose one which looked nice and comfy and had cake and coffee but there were still three hours to go, so we went back to our car and settled, as the rain had increased in volume.

As we were dozing, we noticed a lady unlocking the parish hall door and entering. Immediately, I followed her in and introduced myself. She was the caretaker and had arrived to set up the hall for the ladies and put the chairs out, put the heating on etc. She very kindly invited us in, as she didn't think we should have to sit outside in the car, for which we were grateful.

The caretaker told us to make ourselves comfortable and she only lived three doors away. If there was a problem, just knock on her door.

We used the time to carry everything in and spend some time setting up and making everything look nice and professional, an opportunity we rarely got.

Having put the talk together and being satisfied that we could do no better, we went back to our café and had another cake and another coffee and enjoyed the ambiance and the comfort and warmth.

As the time was approaching for my talk, we made our way back to the parish hall only to find all our props and books and photos, everything we had meticulously arranged, in the refuse bin area all over the place in the rain.

I rushed into the hall where a woman came straight up to me and started apologising to me, saying that she had already been in touch with the primary and nursery schools that share the hall and left them in no doubt of her anger at seeing that they had not cleared away their stuff, enabling the WI to have their meeting and more importantly, allowing the speaker the room to display and set up for the evening.

I looked at her in dismay but owing to the state she was in and taking into consideration that she was acting on our behalf; I was careful in my response.

Quietly and with restraint, I explained that she had just thrown out all my props, photographs, visual aids, merchandise, stool and all my rather valuable display pieces which had taken me years to put together and that everything was now in the refuse compound by the side of the building in the pouring rain which my wife was battling against to retrieve, attempting to save our livelihood.

The woman stared at me in disbelief and I thought she was about to collapse, so I relented a little and dampened my attack and anger, to make things easier.

Annie was rushing in and out soaked to the skin, retrieving what she could and trying to dry things off, hanging important matters over the radiators. As she was doing so some of the women were helping themselves to things they assumed had just been thrown out and Annie was having to search their bags to get them back.

Due to Annie's diligence and speed, along with her care, she got nearly everything back and put together all the items that were not soaked or weather-beaten and we had the semblance of a show to present.

The audience were appreciative and apologetic at what their treasurer had done in error and they all made sure they stayed behind afterwards to make sure all our equipment and goods were back in order and more importantly, back in my car.

Chapter 22

October

Holmfirth WI

Pepsi

When I get invitations to speak at group meetings, the favourite question invariably comes in the guise of a jovial request, "Are you bringing a donkey with you?" or sometimes more seriously, "Will you bring a donkey with you?

One such request arrived in the shape of a lovely poem from a member of a small WI group in Holmfirth, a town I was well acquainted with as half the cast of *Last of the Summer Wine* had supported the welfare of our herd of donkeys for years and been very hands-on with the time and generosity.

I was touched to get the card with the poem inside;

> High in the bleak and beautiful hills
> Surrounded by the limestone grey walls
> There lies a place of shelter and repose
> A sanctuary maintained with loving care
> A welcoming home for donkeys old and
> young, sick or neglected, forlorn or rejected
> Rejuvenated now in friendship and love

In kind weather, the green fields and their
domain in less clement times in the barn they
reside
Their names on the stalls for all to see
With stamping feet and ears pricked high
Their braying voices fill the sky
They munch their treats in noisy bliss
And what a happy sight this is
A holly welcome along the walls
A Christmas tree with coloured lights
Four hopeful donkeys to each stall
With a stocking for gifts pinned on the door
Seats and tables in readiness
For the carol service to be held at night
The air of expectancy is felt by all
There was magic in the barn that day
In the true meaning of Christmas

With love
Mary Marriot

The ladies so enjoyed the experience and
participation that they unanimously voted it the
finest celebration of Christmas they had ever had
together as a group.

I was, quite naturally, very moved by such an
effort of kindness and immediately phoned to thank
her.

"That's how we felt, it was so easy to
compose," she said.

"It means a great deal to me. Thank the ladies for me."

"I will," she said. "But there is one thing they have asked me. When you come to Holmfirth for our annual get together with invited groups from around the area, will you bring a donkey?"

"I will, Mary but I am, at the moment, in the throes of trying to get a French donkey over here who is suffering so much. It's hard work, the journey is financially beyond my present resources but, when I have got him over, I will put my mind to your request and sort something out."

We left it at that, and the weekend went by after which I got another call.

"John, we have had a committee meeting firstly to discuss the forthcoming get together, but which also encompassed your need at present, to bring the donkey over the channel. We want to help. We feel with the help of a couple of members of *Summer Wine*, we may be able to put something together to help you get the donkey over. Will that be alright for us to continue discussing?"

"Of course, let me know if there's anything we can do this end, to help with that idea."

A small French village six miles from Saint Rochelle and a farmhouse with twenty acres of unkept arable land, a paddock on which graze two brown donkeys. The mare is called Cerise and the jack is named Pepsi. The area is a visible tourist trap, typically French, untouched by the hustle and bustle of everyday life. In the village square, the locals gather for their croque monsieur with their news and views of the day's events. Much bread is broken, and many daily problems solved over a tumbler of the best red wine.

Cerise and Pepsi are very much part of village life, respected for their work ethics, which although hard, they both find enjoyable. Their main work consists of taking tourists out for a week's trek around the beautiful countryside pulling a small but efficient gypsy caravan. A lovely little Romany caravan pulled at leisure by two delightful brown donkeys, does life get any better, people ask, they are both always busy. The pair of them appear in more photograph albums than anyone, they receive cards from all over the world. The problems only arise when the holiday makers have to say goodbye to their donkeys.

We have no real idea of how Pepsi felt when he himself had to say goodbye to Cerise as she left him and passed away at the age of thirty but, he went into deep decline. Pepsi would stand alone for days by the fence near the farm kitchen motionless. The owners became worried when he no longer ate and lost a lot of weight. He would not go into his shelter in bad weather as he wasn't prepared to accept the fact that Cerise wasn't there to share it with him.

To make matters worse, his owner developed multiple sclerosis and was finding matters disturbingly difficult, with Cerise's demise and

Pepsi's condition, he had to forgo his only lucrative income and sell the caravans.

I happened to stop at the farm when Annie was making a pilgrimage to the northern Italian town of Assisi with Beethoven, hoping to arrive at the Basilica of Saint Francis on his saint's day. Of course, I was immediately drawn to Pepsi, extremely concerned that the donkey needed serious help to enable him to recover the loss and his health. I learnt also; he was only a teenager.

I made up my mind that I would do all I could to get him home with us. The owner was not only willing to let him go but relieved that Pepsi would have a chance.

The ladies' endeavours came to fruition and they managed to get enough finance and backing to complete the transport transaction and to make Pepsi comfortable for a few months while he settled in.

All the donkeys at the sanctuary have helped children to overcome difficulties, reach ambitions and generally improve their lives: donkeys handing out therapeutic friendship at which they are experts.

Then comes that moment when one donkey stands out, when they bond with someone and start an unbreakable partnership. I have been privileged to have had that very special association.

Pepsi became my donkey overnight. Together we worked and travelled hundreds of miles. He was known at first as my after-dinner donkey.

When I prepared for a talk on my own, I used to gather and sort out all my huge photos. Some of my stories are so incredible, I have found it easier to let the actual photos take the strain. They add authenticity to what I am recounting. Pepsi would be enjoying his tea with his wife Oxo when he would see me putting my photos in the trailer. This was his cue for action. He would kiss the wife goodnight and start thumping on his stable door to be let out for work. I would put on his best leather head collar and choose one of his many coloured coats for the journey.

Pepsi's special coats had all been designed and made by the Holmfirth WI who were showing a huge personal interest in him now. The coats were made of fifty-two-inch squares, all different colours and crocheted for strength. They were unique and he resembled Joseph with his amazing coloured coats. He had coats for all seasons, light coloured dust sheets for the summer, heavy duty woollen ones for the winter months.

I never had to lead Pepsi into the trailer. Without fail, he walked in himself and waited to be tied up by his hay net. He loved it. It felt very much like his own place of work and travel. Each venue was new to him with their different needs. He always adapted without a murmur of discontent, always calm. He was at home in a school assembly hall, a village hut, a church or a hotel banqueting suite, he managed them all professionally and efficiently.

I had to adapt my talk to suit the needs of those I was visiting to entertain but without any consultation, Pepsi would way up the situation for himself and often choose where it would be best for him to be, so everybody got a good view of him. He had his own floor covering, a tarpaulin which the ladies had painted country scenes on, mainly of Holmfirth, just in case of accidents. But I can honestly say that in the eight years we travelled together, he never let me down.

If we were in a gymnasium or on a parquet floor, the ladies had made him a pair of boots so that he didn't scratch any surfaces.

There were moments during the talk when I needed him to react. For these moments, we did have a lengthy rehearsal period, but he got it in the end and when it all finally fitted into place for him, he never forgot what he was supposed to do. He didn't need telling twice.

I would look at him and ask him if he was ready for a polo mint. He would nod and I would ask a lady in the audience to do the honours. He would accept the polo and always nod thanking her for her treat. It took three months of daily effort and hundreds of polos to get him to do that, but the clever bit was, he would never ask for a second one. I was fortunate that polo actually sponsored him, so we were never short of mints.

Pepsi worked the London Palladium, Great Ormond Street Hospital for sick children, the Savoy

Hotel, a meeting with the Queen at Buckingham Place and some very prestigious venues up and down the country. He visited dozens of children's hospices, school libraries, over three hundred WI's, plus inner wheels, rotaries, British Lions, gold clubs etc.

When Pepsi passed away, I gave up touring our talk, 'Marked for Life', I just couldn't go on stage without him, it was too painful. My association with Pepsi has always been a reminder of how hard double acts work and inspire each other. There was never going to be a way to recapture what we had, and I had to come to terms with that. Pepsi raised thousands of pounds over his short career, it's doubtful without his integrity and the women of Holmfirth and their faith in him, whether the sanctuary would ever have got on to a firm footing as I did. I can assure you all that not one day goes by when I don't think of that donkey, his affection and his smile.

A short while after Pepsi passed away, another poem came through the post, this time from a special needs teenager which I have framed and keep in a very prominent place and I would like to share it with you, as she was an extraordinary child.

"I've written this for your lad, just throw it away if it's no good," she wrote.

After straightening the crumpled piece of paper I read it and I have been reading it every Christmas in all the cathedrals and churches ever since Pepsi's ladies in Holmfirth turned it into a sampler which is absolutely out of this world and the young lady was able to see it before she passed away.

Chapter 24

October

Ingrave WI

In search of a new home

I have been known, in my time, to be the last production company in the theatre that is closing but, to be invited to do my talk for a WI hall that is closing down is a new one. It makes me think that on my travels, I have been to many groups who are unable to carry on, mainly through lack of membership but now we have the village halls and church halls needing extra cash to keep them open and the local councils seem to be making a big drive for the village hall and other distinctive venues laid aside, until now, for the Women's Institutes.

The more fortunate groups of WI's own their own halls and have done for years, thus able to run them with a reasonable subscription, but once again, arriving at Ingrave, I listen to the president's address and the fact that once again, the local body of those who make the decisions, have invited a pre-nursery school to take over on a weekday basis which will naturally increase the income and make the hall more viable, leaving the Women's Institute to vacate a property they have been in for over a hundred years.

There is both a question of leadership and on the other hand, a lack of interested people participating. It seemed to me, as an onlooker, that at Ingrave, there was a resolute acceptance that they could not argue the point that they were, in fact, just playing out the years in accepting that they had had occupancy for a century that it could no longer last. The ladies were invited to two other venues to see which of them they preferred to have their future meetings in, even though the president felt neither was suitable there was little choice. I have been present in so many school assembly halls of an evening, gymnasiums or a nursery school, not as many church halls but some extremely pleasant well designed and modern halls that make up the county requirements for the ladies.

There is, without a shadow of a doubt, a vibrancy in some of the more modern and well-designed halls with some very good quality accessories to make an interesting evening go even better and above all, to make the women who attend to have enjoyed not just the evening but the surroundings as well.

The intentions of the Ingrave group were without exception, noble in intent. Hundreds of teddy bear puppets and woollen animals festooned all around the hall being delivered to stroke units, children's hospices, disabled centres and so many other outlets. Does the local authority think this is unimportant as a pre-school set up? Could the two not be combined together, leaving the WI its normal one day a month and allowing the education all the rest of the month?

In my capacity as a theatre producer, there are some dates which you can't wait to take your productions to, in the knowledge that you will have a good week both financially, artistically and because the place is vibrant, it is well run and above all, the vibrancy is effective and travels from the workers associated to the audience who support and enjoy.

This, I can identify completely with, on my WI travels around the country and now with over five-hundred talks under my belt, it is possible to make comparisons. When I reach the Surrey Federation, I am faced with, for instance, the Bookham Belles, a youngish but vibrant group, where it is even difficult to talk because so much interesting and enthusiastic stuff has gone before you but whose audience are fantastic, mainly due to their enthusiasm and future assessments and now they have, in only a year or two, off-shoots, the Bookham Bees and the Bookham Butterflies, all with long waiting lists which they have had to enforce. Maybe these successful groups should impart some of their outlooks and ideas and schemes to the less fortunate and struggling groups, or even share their venues?

Of course, there is the age question which should never be an issue, a standard to be met, to be kept in compliance with their federations quite understandably, utmost and unique, well tested and successful formats so, at that stage, let's not forget the *Calendar Girls* who went against their superiors and their federation and threw themselves into the twentieth century and made the biggest impact that the Women's Institute have had for as long as can be remembered. Some groups even followed their example and copied the format. The stage shows followed all around the country, giving the federation more publicity than had ever been achieved or dreamt of before, the film finished it off with a brilliant cast, the effect was astonishing. But I still hear at the less forward thinking group meetings that they hit the establishment with something uncharacteristic and in some quarters, still challenged and questioned as unorthodox which has been able to give the WI a new image which does not altogether qualify with their charitable stance.

To answer that query, you have to look at what the project actually raised in cash and spirit and what benefit one of the worst diseases we have had to endure gained from their marvellous attempt, I believe the question answers itself, the women were wonderful, brave and committed, all the qualities that the organisation embodied over the last century.

When my president, June Brown MBE, then in her middle eighties, informed me that she was going to go into the West End production of *Calendar Girls*, I applauded her courage.

Not needing the money, also at the same time, having to film weekly episodes of *EastEnders,* she didn't need to do it but she wanted to and appearing at the Wyndham Theatre in the heart of the West End, all her friends coming to see her was hard for her but she did it as much for the cause as for the success.

June Brown has been to many of my WI meetings with me as we ran a successful charity for both children and rescue donkeys and women always ask her whether she minded taking her clothes off at her age. She always answers the question by saying if my charity had the chance to do what those ladies have done for theirs, we would be overjoyed and grateful for ever. There's your answer.

When I talk, I witness so much dementia and in my programme, I broach the subject through Patricia Hayes the actress and Barbara Windsor who have both suffered so greatly in the knowledge that those two women were decorated three times each for their charitable work and their endeavours were started when they were all in middle age towards the end of their lives. The three of them had to turn so many corners and change so many attitudes, listen so hard to what the youth was saying, what the modern world was expecting, going forward needs that impetus and the church halls to need it to.

I always listen carefully to the women who have been in the groups for years, I learn and I digest what went on and how they dealt with it but then I listen to the other side of the coin and the mothers with young children and their definitions and there is little room for looking back to their beginnings, they just look forward to try and make sure all is well for their children.

I have listened to hundreds of presidents' speeches, some have inspired me, some have made me laugh, some have filled me with their sense of humour which they so cleverly translate to their congregations. Then there are a few who convey disapproval, who chastise the women for not coming forward to make up committees, who get really angry at the subscriptions that for whatever reason haven't been handed in on the requested day. Two different approaches but two feelings which generate confidence and enthusiasm against a tiresome and repeatedly boring meeting.

I have been lucky, having been able to have such special votes of thanks, having great evenings with a wonderful group of inspiring women, but against that, I listen and I hear that there have been many speakers who have not quite got their attention. I heard from a lady in her eighties at Ingrave who for me, summed the whole system up in a nutshell.

"The ones who are boring and uninteresting, go on for too long, always so keen to hear the sound of their own voice and then there are those who are brilliant and we would wish for more but they sensibly know exactly when to stop, leaving everybody happy."

I try to give the group both sides of the coin which I believe is important. Nostalgia at the beginning, hoping that the young ones will recognise and appreciate the past and then into the charitable side and the modern way, in which all the actors and actresses have addressed the times we're in, the needs we require for it are the same in the theatre world, they have to keep abreast with the times. The theatres themselves have to adapt to the needs of the audiences, they have to refurnish to a comfortable and modern standard, so everyone is comfortable. We are all basically in the same game, but we have to work hard to maintain its quality and its standard otherwise, they won't come to see us, any of us.

Chapter 25

November

Menai Straits WI

An island paradise

Anglesey has always been one of our favourite destinations for a short break or even in the summer, a day out. We can reach the island within two hours and it's always a smooth motorway run from our home although we try and avoid the peak summer months due to the heavy traffic and packed beaches. Our ideal preferences are from April to the end of May or end of September to early November. This small piece of paradise offers up everything we require and yearn for and often more.

Annie and I have explored the island extensively and come up with some ideal hideaways and stunning views, incomparable coves and beaches that on a good day just blow your mind away and get my creative juices flowing. Both our Cypriot terriers made this their favourite place to go mad and enjoy themselves, second only to Cornwall which they seem to associate with Cyprus. The favourite family beach for the four of us has always been without exception, Newborough Beach, the most fantastic stretch of sand flanked by a panoramic view of the entire Snowdonia mountain range which encompasses the bay with an extraordinary effect and leaves one breathless. The beach itself is perfect and always clean, no plastic, no rubbish, always maintained with care and precision.

A walk of around a mile along the stretch of sand and one reaches the old lighthouse and pilot cottages, still very much intact and facing the Irish sea, although no longer operational, still painted brilliant white, so enhancing their surroundings. There's always time for reflection and our flask of warm coffee or soup depending which month we choose to be there. Seals heads appear frequently near to the shore and the small man-made harbour obviously favoured for overnight stays when the public vacated their home.

It is with all this in mind that I was determined to do some business and find out more about the locals and their history on the island, so I made a move to ask if I could talk to the Menai Straits WI. At first, the response was tepid, it seemed nobody had ever asked to actually go there, and a committee meeting would have to be put together to deal with this alien request.

First to come back to me was the programme organiser who was lukewarm about the idea, but after listening, said she would take it to their next committee meeting and gauge what the reaction was, although she was not holding out much hope, even though I had tried to sell myself hard, which it seemed, had had an adverse effect, as I was seemingly far too expensive for their budget, "We never pay more than thirty pounds."

I tried not to show any surprise or disappointment, quickly having worked out in my head that this amount would not even cover the petrol to get there, I smiled and shrugged my shoulders in acceptance. This acceptance seemed to wrong-foot the organiser, used to having to battle for tea money on more than one occasion but she seemed to me to be warming to the idea a little more in the knowledge that this fool was willing to come a long way for a somewhat poultry sum, in fact at his own expense. This would make it a lot easier at the next committee meeting.

"Have you any leaflets or publicity?" I handed both over and she read them a little in disbelief at what she had in front of her.

"You have been speaker of the year?

"Yes."

"You have spent time at Buckingham Palace with the queen?"

"Yes."

"You have acted and produced all these people and shows?"

"Yes."

"And you want to come to us and give a talk called, *Toytown to Buckingham Palace*? Where does Toytown come into it?"

"Enid Blyton chose me to play Noddy on stage."

She stared at me wondering whether I was pulling her bells.

"Really?"

"Yes."

After a pause, "Well, I will put it to the committee, and you will accept thirty pounds?"

"Yes."

That was the meeting over. She didn't really leave me with any impression whether she thought it was a good idea or not just that if she could pull this off for thirty pounds, she might get a couple of Brownie points with those who matter.

When I got home, I got a call from her asking if I could go down and meet her president and see what she thought, just for a coffee locally. Although this was another sixty pounds in petrol, I was still determined to crack this group and I went down with Annie and we had another lovely walk along Newborough Beach, and I met the president in an upmarket restaurant.

"Mr Stirling, I have read your extensive web site and you seem to have had a very wonderful and varied career. What I can't understand is why you want to come down here at basically your own cost?" I managed to explain to her my desire to spend more time on the island and I was trying to find things and people to make it all come together. She stared at me and ordered a croissant which I got the impression I was going to be asked to pay for." Right, well I've got enough now to put it to the committee, and I'll let you know," and that was that.

Six months went by and by the time the programme organiser actually got back to me, I had forgotten that I'd even asked to go there. I had, in that time, already done Bangor University, Llandudno's Rotary Christmas dinner, an evening at Colwyn Bay theatre etc.

The voice on the phone said, "I am the programme secretary for the Menai Straits."

"Oh, I'm sorry I can't come down again for another meeting."

"No," she said, "That won't be necessary, we have decided to go ahead with it, if you are available."

She gave me a date and we agreed on terms. I did try and say petrol had increased in price since my last meeting, but this fell on deaf ears and I realised I was on a losing wicket and it was now time to get this over with.

We drove down on the allocated day, as Annie had set her heart on a cruise to Puffin Island before the talk, to make sense of the journey. We arrived to find the tide was out, so the boat couldn't go until tomorrow. We decided then to go to our favourite Bistro in Red Wharf Bay for an afternoon tea but alas, the lack of public meant that the owner had closed early, so we just hung around Menai Strait, waiting for the evening.

I had been given directions to the Catholic hall where the group meets, and we found it easily. It was a typical WI hall and strangely, the front door was open, so Annie and I took advantage of our luck and moved all the props in and set up for the evening talk, it took us about four minutes. We went for a coffee and returned fifteen minutes before I was supposed to talk, only to find we had set up in the Royal Air

Force cadet hut and they were about to play indoor five-a-side football. They instructed me where we supposed to be, and we rushed like mad to take it all down and hurry next door where the actual meeting was just about to start.

"You're rather late," announced the president rather harshly, "But we put it down to the traffic."

We didn't say or react to her address, just quickly got on with preparing the talk for the second time in two hours.

"I am just going to give a short address and cover a small bit of business and then hand over to you."

One hour a five minutes later, she introduced me.

The president had been surprised by how many women had turned up and brought guests, so she had used this larger-than-usual ensemble to go for it and give a special performance.

As I started, I was alarmed by a woman who kept standing up every five minutes, crossing the hall in front of me and putting her head round the kitchen door and just standing there for a few minutes then returning to her seat. On the third such crossing, I stopped and asked her if there was something wrong and she explained.

"We share the hall, Mr Stirling, with the AA group who talk in the next room and as they are local alcoholics, they don't want us to know who they are, and we share the kitchen for teas and cakes you see, and I have to check every so often if they are having their tea break, so as to know when I can go in and put the kettle on." So, I battled on with the lady making frequent extra crossings.

Nearing the end of the talk, I heard a very heavy pair of footsteps coming up the wooden stairs into the hall and a vision of a woman completely covered in scalfs with a very large hat and nothing of her visible, except for her eyes, which were strangely staring ahead.

As no-one seemed wanting to know what she wanted, it rested with me to ask.

"Can we help you?"

"I hope so. I can't get my car out of the car park. I am blocked in. Could the person with Citroen YMC17 OPC please move it now?"

As my wife can't drive, I had to go down and move it, in case the person looking like an Egyptian mummy's bandages came down and we actually saw who she was, which could have led to future problems for her and the community.

I finally had earned my thirty pounds and was told it was the best talk they had ever had. This made me wonder what they had had to endure for so many years, as it was certainly not my finest hour with all the interruptions but I got what I wanted out of it and Annie sold a good deal of merchandise from which she had to give them ten percent.

We still adore Anglesey; we have made some friends through the talk, which is lovely and our experience with the North Wales WI was a joy and amusing to look back on.

Later, I received from the Menai Straits WI another very positive report, one reproduced in full in the appendices at the back of the book.

Chapter 26

December

Great Longstone WI

Nativity time

I have always felt a certain amount of shame as we near the season of goodwill that I have been unable or simply have not made the time and effort to acknowledge and participate in local Christmas celebrations of immense importance to the small and important villages surrounding our farm and country.

I can find a certain solace in the fact that the approaching yuletide coincides with a hugely busy time for us with children's Christmas parties. This includes our own annual carol concert which tends to dominate our thoughts and time, especially decorating our barn. This space, which could hold a Cathay Pacific jumbo jet with room to spare, seems to take our creative endeavours and spare hours to conceive but, with the help of three window dressers from two of the leading stores in Manchester, we manage to get there with little time to spare. To embellish thirty-three stables, hang large Christmas stockings on every donkey's door, kindly donated each year by the Great Longstone WI, is a ritual we love. We did, however, encounter problems the first year, as we filled the stockings prematurely to the brim with polo mints which we learnt from our mistake was foolhardy, as the occupants emptied them entirely as soon as lights were turned out for bedtime.

I got a great number of requests each year, from places near and far to make their nativity presentations and productions come alive, requesting the inclusion of a real donkey, giving the whole proceedings that certain essential authenticity and magic. I was always sad that I was unable to comply or accept their kind invitations so this year, I had made up my mind that I would put things to one side, make a real effort to take part wholeheartedly in giving a village a donkey to bring their efforts to life. I chose the village of Great Longstone as the women of the village had done so much for me over the years. The donkeys would not have the pleasure of their stockings, their lovely Christmas coats or blankets, were it not for these heroic silver foxes. So, it was definitely time for me to join in and assist this lovely small community to have something to remember. I decided that I would take six donkeys so that the smaller children, who did not have Mary's credentials on the night with her own mount, could also enjoy a similar experience without having to go the same distance as our Mary. A journey from Jerusalem to Bethlehem would have tested my animals' feelings of affection to the extreme. On this occasion, the children would have to make do with a gentler and less demanding route from Little Longstone to Great Longstone, a journey of a mile but enough to make the five donkeys wish they hadn't been chosen.

It was agreed that the nativity would be built in a farm on the outskirts of the village in the corner of a courtyard which had a certain appeal. An old barn of some local notoriety with historic value, it was best the children weren't informed about its daily practice of preparing cows and sheep for slaughter and assisting in complicated births which quite a few animals had to deal with. The vicar had blessed the ground in advance and the ladies of Great Longstone would not only undertake the decoration of the holy stable, but they would also officiate in bringing the church to the required status for the Christmas mass which would follow.

The path was set aside for the procession to take place with all its shepherds, kings and village dignitaries. For some reason because they had the costumes and didn't want to waste them, there would be a representation of Roman centurions. A new one on most of us, but hopefully, one which would enthral us all. However, the organisers had failed to research that at the back of the farm, directly in the path of this important track, was an abattoir which was extremely busy twenty-four hours a day. I was loath to explain that the donkeys would probably not go through that area as the smell would alarm them, possibly even make them feel they were being led to their deaths which I was quite sure was not the envisaged purpose of this festive occasion. After three committee meetings, it was agreed that the procession would have to take the required route but, the children who were riding the donkeys, would be allowed to take an alternative route through the graveyard.

The barn would be filled with bales of hay which I explained again, that in my opinion, the public would have to take their seats pretty quickly, as six donkeys could defeat the public arrangements without the slightest hesitation. I got the impression, as every time they made a suggestion and I found reason to oppose it, things were not running as smoothly as they could have done. They were all beginning to wonder, and the general consensus was, that maybe the Longstone ladies, although totally revered and respected, had on this occasion, perhaps dropped a clanger approaching me with my beasts of burden.

The farmer went to great lengths to advise and insist that all the public, children included, wore Wellington boots on the night, as he had no option but to slurry all his fields the day before the spectacle. Otherwise, everybody would be knee deep in rather pungent cow muck. Although he would recommend it all at times for those with sinus and respiratory conditions, others might find it unpleasant, especially as the women of Longstone were intending a feast of food, cakes etc, to be served in the barn.

The farmer thought it would be prudent that he take all the muck away and spread it in the neighbouring village fields. I couldn't start to imagine what the people of the neighbouring community would think, how it might spoil their more quiet and respectful celebrations. The farmer insisted all would be well as he would invite most of them to come. The only absentee would be the pig farmer as he wouldn't be able to leave the animals as all his sows and piglets would be indoors at that time which many of us thought was probably the best news we had received that day.

At the December monthly meeting of the Great Longstone's Women's Institute, the nativity took pride of place with certain excitement and anticipation of grandeur and expectation. They had invited all the villagers who had helped in organising the event; I was to give my talk, followed by a finger buffet.

It was a jolly evening, the women were in good form, the pig farmer had turned up, he needed no introduction. The women were able to secure him a special place for himself and his wife, so they too could enjoy the evening just far away enough to be acceptable.

It was agreed that all was going to plan, that the costumes were all done and their thanks went out to my Annie for assisting in that department saving the day with her expertise. The choir gave a resounding attempt to perform the hymn they were going to sing on the night, the head teacher reassuring us at the end of it that, although there was still some work to be done, it would be alright on the night. How often have I heard that?

One disturbing motion was passed this time, I managed to keep my own council and didn't interfere or make any kind of suggestion. A local farmer's wife, who lived near the barn, had just given birth to a baby boy who was now just five weeks old and she was keen to donate him for the crib, as the baby Jesus. I was praying and hoping indeed that someone in authority would question the wisdom of this generous offer but, in my estimation foolhardy suggestion, as for all intents and purposes, there were going to be a few animals surrounding the crib at given moments in the proceedings, a large overbearing cow accompanied by an untrained goat plus the donkey with ducks and geese having also been thrown in for good measure. All this, in my estimation, would make it a little precarious, if not dangerous, for an eight-week old baby, however beautiful and real, to be in that situation. His mother affirmed she would place him in the basket just before it all began and not be far away in case of trouble. But no-one spoke or voiced an opinion.

The women's main concerns revolved around the weather conditions which were on that evening's news bulletin and extremely poor with high winds and gales combined with heavy rain in all areas. The decision was made unanimously that the nativity should go ahead.

The rain arrived as expected and predicted but a little harder than anticipated. The farmer had fought hard spreading his slurry, getting bogged down many times in his tractor, so many times, in fact, that the entrance to the courtyard and the barn were practically impassable or inaccessible.

A large crowd arrived with galoshes and Wellington boots as suggested, ready for the onslaught the weather was going to impose on them. They seemed valiantly undaunted, ready to celebrate correctly the birth of our lord who had arrived in his buggy and was suitably attired in a white baby-grow to make the whole thing very real.

The cow had been cast alongside the donkey and the goat had not had time to be milked that evening which happened like clockwork each day at five, so she was understandably fractious and uncooperative, feeling uncomfortable with her load. Unable to lie down or assume the required position, she also voiced her opinions which woke the baby in the buggy which the mother had meticulously put to sleep with an overdose of pure milk directly from the breast so as to be sure he slept through his forthcoming ordeal. This was now not to be, it looked like the mother was having to dress up in disguise to be able to take a position by the crib, assuming the role of an aged governess to our creator.

The choir gave a spirited performance against the wind and gales which somewhat muffled the effect but, the audience showed a genuine appreciation of the work and trouble put into rehearsing such an ecclesiastical masterpiece. There was quite obviously, a huge well of sympathy for the teacher who had devoted six months to get them to this standard, but she looked as if she might try again next year.

Pepsi was the only animal to stand still for the required time, the cow had long gone and made her own way to the milking shed, the goat had to be released as he was getting dangerous and there was the threat of someone being gored. Although the ducks didn't mean any harm, they disappeared as the farmer's wife thought she was doing right by installing a baby's paddling pool outside the kitchen door and that's where they all promptly went. To the delight of the audience, one chicken actually laid an egg in public, making it the high point of the night.

The vicar and the ladies saved the night. A brilliant sermon and a story for the children elevated the vicar to archbishop status for the night while the women enthralled the gathering with an impressive bell-ringing session which was much enjoyed and very much in keeping with the time of year.

The teas were splendid and the cakes much admired. On the whole it was a night to remember. For some of us, it had its moments. The donkeys had been led through the abattoir which had the desired effect and were re-captured after an extensive chase.

Happy Christmas ladies, well done.

Chapter 27

December

Wath Upon Dearn WI

Blessed Kojak

Four o'clock in the afternoon, we are just settling down comfortably and snuggly for a long-awaited tea. The dogs didn't want to venture outside for their usual early evening sniff and more important matters, so they too, have hit the basket next to the two-bar electric fire which in these extreme winter conditions, adds a helpful hand to bolster the central heating, which is at full blast.

Snow is falling outside as the telephone rings in the hall. A Churchillian voice on the other end is shouting at me as if my hearing is impaired.

"Mr Stirling, you are my last hope." Reminiscent of the beach landings.

"Our speaker has pulled out due to adverse conditions, I have tried several others to see if they could help but none of them seem keen to venture out this evening."

I was just going to intervene to say that I had much sympathy with their wise decision when she came battling back.

"One of our members said you came in a land rover a week ago and got through, so I am asking if you could oblige tonight?"

This did not grab me as exciting under the circumstances. I was not at all keen to comply with this one. When I asked the exact location, it was Wath Upon Dearn in West Yorkshire, a pretty but nonetheless rugged area, flanked on all sides by the Yorkshire moors and National Park which had already appeared on the news recently as unpassable.

"Would you not consider a cancellation in this instance as more prudent?" I asked, hoping she might accept this advice.

"The ladies are adamant they want to proceed. It's our Christmas gathering."

"I asked the lady politely for a few minutes to consult my wife who would have to make this perilous journey with me, not only as an intricate part of my talk, but in case of any recoveries that might have to be administered on route.

Annie's attitude was that we should just get on with our toad-in-the-hole which would be far more beneficial than a dangerous expedition into the unknown from which we might never return. However, after the lady in question had mentioned a refusal might go down badly with future Yorkshire requests (a desperation was now taking a hold on her), I decided I would try.

Fortunately, I had put snow tyres on that week.

We loaded the land rover with our props, blankets, shovel, hot flask of Bovril, breakdown light and roadside breakdown triangle and in case we had to stay the night in unforeseen circumstances, a duvet. Daunted by the prospect of a tough journey ahead, we slowly crept away from a comfortable bungalow radiating heat and comfort, skidding carefully along our road and on to a deserted A6.

Within a mile, we realised we were in a hazardous situation but there was no turning back. Annie had the map on her lap as our navigational aid would not register the weather conditions and would insist on the holiday route, which was impassable, so we had to judge it for ourselves and make decisions she was incapable of. The pretty route and the holiday route were now totally out of the question, neither were valid in this Antarctic blizzard.

We ploughed through the Peak District National Park noticing that we were totally alone. We got through Sheffield, just, on to a snow-bound Rotherham, then the land rover was put to the ultimate test. If we were to believe the salesman who sold her to us, we might get through, but we were at present not totally convinced.

The satnav indicated Barnsley was the way forward, so Annie decided on Hoyland, which seemed nearer to our destination. She got us there and then across the moors, towards Wath Upon Dearn itself.

A two-hour journey was now in its fourth hour and slowing as we went. I had been directed by the lady that it was a WI hut of sorts, basically on a high ridge which sounded awkward and better than the reality of its position which was, in fact, on the top of a mountain, a small mountain but a mountain, nevertheless.

At this point, our shovel came out of the boot and Annie was preparing to phone our dog sitter to let her know she was in for the night and to bunker down but the remoteness of our position meant there was no signal for the phone.

We finally got to the sign welcoming us to Wath Upon Dearn with an AA van, its light flashing for us to stop. Even though the site of him was encouraging, it seemed as if he had himself broken down. If he couldn't go on, what chance had we?

He asked us where we were heading for? We gave him the postcode for the hut.

"Are you mad?" he said.

"Listen, if you can tow me back two miles, I will explain where things are and the best way for you both to get through."

We hooked him up and we got him moving again. As we towed, he was able to re-start his frozen engine. After sharing our Bovril, he actually volunteered to escort us to the venue which we thought immensely kind or stupid, we couldn't decide which. Fortunately, I was able to produce my AA card which he said was invaluable when he reported the incident back to base. It indicated I was a fully paid up member, thank god.

Eventually, looking like three people who had scaled the Himalayas, we arrived at what was indeed a garden hut. We battled our way in to be greeted by three elderly ladies sat around a Calor gas stove crocheting. They looked up rather bemused at our entrance and to see them with blankets over their laps, they were obviously prepared for a lock-down of sorts which, in itself, would be fairly daunting in this very confined space.

"What are you doing here?" the lady said, dropping a stitch.

"I've come to give you a talk," I explained shrugging off half a ton of snow from my coat and Annie's back.

"We aren't expecting a talk; it's not Thursday," she said angrily with the two other ladies agreeing in unison.

"Are you mad in this weather?"

An immediate nod of approval was voiced by my two travelling companions, although Annie was perhaps a trifle more hostile and had an edge on the placid but worried AA man.

I explained that having crossed the Antarctic and brought everything with us, it would seem a shame not to actually go through with it. The three of them seemed to have difficulty with this reasoning.

"We have a better idea," she said, after they had conferred for a few minutes.

The three of us looked bemused at this suggestion. Had it been a lovely sunny and warm evening drive of a lifetime over some of the prettiest country in England with a mug of tea on a garden bench outside their garden hut, overlooking outstanding views of the Yorkshire dales and moors, we might have laughed and seen the funny side of it all. But as it was, the AA man had forgone his dinner, my wife was nursing chilblains, I was attempting to deal with an asthmatic condition brought on by high altitude and cold winds, so we were not ready, or equipped, for jovial levity at this exact stage of the proceedings.

The women carried on crocheting but seemed now to momentarily accept that we had come a long way under difficult circumstances, so they succumbed to the fact that I was there to give them a talk.

So it was, that I addressed the smallest WI in my short career as a speaker. It actually went well, with the AA man lapping it up, especially the celebrity input. The ladies enjoyed the donkey rescue stories, even though Annie noticed they never looked up at the photos and never even dropped a stitch as I waffled on. By the time I finished my talk, she estimated they had nearly finished a blanket.

I always close my talk on an anecdote about the actor Brian Blessed who has been so kind and generous to our cause for a long time, but this evening, the story brought an amazing revelation that I was not expecting.

Brian had come to the Blackpool Pleasure Beach to support a fundraising evening for the donkeys and the children but he had, during the day, visited the beach donkeys and been told how they had just rescued a stallion who they could not have on the beach for obvious reasons, as his manhood would get in the way of the gentle backwards and forwards, stick-to-stick walk the donkeys were trained to do.

Brian was intrigued by the stallion whose name was Kojak. He was a very tall donkey at fifteen hands in height and muscular, in accordance with his gender.

Brian asked if we would take the stallion in. He would support his man, as he put it, always keen to support animals but also keen to support this magnificent beast with manhood intact; that seemed to mean a great deal to Brian, his attitude of strength and power, the way masculinity is interpreted through strength and adventures, something he has himself never been short of. Kojak's manhood was of huge importance to him, the donkey's shape and prowess in certain departments had to be revered and kept intact.

After three weeks of having brought Kojak to our sanctuary, I received a call from America where Brian was filming, a friendly call to see how Kojak was behaving and getting on.

"Do you want the good news Brian, or the bad news first," I asked.

"Oh god, the bad news."

Nervously, I informed him of the situation in hand.

"I have castrated your donkey."

I said it as firmly as I could, realising there was going to be a backlash and in the knowledge that this news was not going to be accepted normally or quietly.

Brian Blessed is renowned for speaking his mind and not holding back on matters he disagrees with and so I got it with both barrels smoking. It wasn't a pleasant half-hour, and on this occasion, he wasn't his usual friendly self. In fact, to put it mildly, he went berserk.

"What's the bloody good news then?" he said, trying to maintain a certain civility towards me in the knowledge that I would always do what was best for his actual animal.

"I've kept them for you."

As I concluded this short anecdote which had amused only the AA man, who could hardly refrain himself from laughing out loud, one of the ladies dropped her crotchet needles and started to cough uncontrollably. The other two companions had to brave the outside weather conditions and help her walk around the hut with caution on the ice. They walked her around three times before bringing her back to the Calor gas stove and the warmth.

They sat her down. She carried on coughing for a while and was getting what seemed in an awful state.

"Brian is her son, Mr Stirling."

With this news, the AA man fell off his chair in mirth. Even Annie had thought that it had made such an intrepid journey worthwhile.

When you undertake something which you feel is worthy of the effort or indeed, too much trouble to undertake, one should always think back. Yes, it was a silly journey to make. Yes, they didn't especially want me to talk. Yes, I put my wife, myself and the AA man in a somewhat dangerous position but I always remember my mother's motto in life, "You have to reach the top of the hill and look back to see how far you've come."

I have dined out on that story for some years now, Mrs Blessed never forgot, and Brian was amused by the outcome. I'm not saying it made him forgive me for what I did to Kojak who has now remained with me for many years, calmer, happier and not always thinking of things we wouldn't allow him to do.

As for the talk, they gave me thirty pounds which was the norm, in case they hadn't got any more on them. All three had to get their purses out to make it up.

I never got a letter of thanks, but I got much more. When I returned nine months later and faced the entire Wath Upon Dearn WI, all eighteen of them, I was presented with a lovely crocheted blanket for Kojak and he now wears his coat of many colours on special occasions and children's parties.

Thanks ladies, it was a pleasure.

Epilogue

Falmouth

My secret retirement

Until now, age has been of little concern to me, just numbers that roll forward of little consequence, it was only some four years ago that some brave person who I must have been well acquainted with mentioned the notion of retirement which took me by surprise as I can honestly say I had given it little thought and was of little interest to me. Like many of my generation, my mentality was still reflecting that of my school days, but I had to admit that physically, things were perhaps becoming a little more strenuous than I would have wished for.

Living in an idyllic but isolated rural setting with only hills and dales surrounding us, not a house or telegraph pole in sight, was to be envied. In the summer months, we spent much time on our bench on the terrace, surrounded by beasts of burden and affectionate Cypriot terriers. However, the winter months were unavoidable. We could not get away from the strong winds, the interminable rain and the cold. Also, mucking out seventy donkeys who needed a lot of attention, plus a days' work introducing or writing were seemingly, taking their toll.

Annie was also running a tearoom which had become very popular with queues at the weekend. She was working with children with special needs and her dressmaking and designs needed attention so, she too, was feeling the pressure of time and motion.

I decided reaching our seventies that I had to consider not retiring but making a move in another direction. Retiring from one situation would enable us to venture on in another direction with the same effort, enthusiasm and work ethic but perhaps more in keeping with our physical capabilities.

I decided that not only was the time moving but it was possible, after twenty-nine years, that we might not be as forward thinking or modernised to cope with the vast alterations that life was throwing up at us. It made me realise that perhaps someone younger with new ideas would be more beneficial. However, I found it impossible to attract a responsible couple or person to take over the mantle. There were plenty of animal lovers who wanted nothing less than a chance to work with rescued donkeys but that was only a small part of the work. Getting up at six in the morning in all weathers, mucking out, land husbandry, exercising the animals, preparing them for an arduous day with children who needed a good deal of special attention and of course, for remuneration, a salary which itself was not that attractive but the important statistic in keeping a vulnerable charity going. The plus sides were the farmhouse, nicely decorated and maintained over the years, a lovely home in expansive grounds, a car supplied by the trust, a weekly maintenance fee for food and general supplies required for country-style living. to the sanctuary. But my problem was that no-one came forward.

Then one morning, I received a call from Judy Giles, phoning me from Cornwall, wanting to ask me for advice. She was running a small but important donkey foundation, in a small village outside Truro, which her mother had created some years earlier before passing away and leaving the whole thing for Judy to sort out and take over. Judy had researched all relevant donkey sanctuaries before making the call. She had chosen me as a preferred start for her questions and help, due to my successful means of raising the necessary charitable funds.

Her major bete noir was fundraising, never being able to raise enough money to keep things ticking over and with the relentless introduction of needy donkeys on a weekly basis, things were getting fraught and desperate (I knew the feeling).

Judy had chosen me due to the fact that my strength appeared to be in that quarter. It seemed that every month, I had something going on to compensate for the lack of donations and general public contributions. How could she set about it? More importantly, could I advise her on how to do it? I was quick to explain that my case was different, as I worked with a circle of actors and actresses, performers who gave me an insight into their vulnerabilities and equally important, jobs. I was also an employer, so I was in a position to employ. I interested people in projects which I considered to their advantage and mine. I hate to think, if I had not been in that position, how I would have raised money, because I soon learnt that you have to actually face the relevant celebrities face-to-face in order to interest them. Once you have their individual attention, you are then able to entice them to help. It was normally hard work but beneficial. The generosity among busy, talented artists was sublime but for an outsider, there were the agents and managers to deal with, people who were employed for the sole purpose of dealing with the millions of requests asked of their clients and it was very rare for anyone from outside to get past them.

One has to realise that there is no financial benefit for anyone in helping charities. For the managers, there is no commission and no incentive other than gaining the respect from their clients for their diligence and competence in dealing with matters and relieving them of the necessity of looking selfish and hard in saying no, or refusing to attend well-deserved causes in need of their time.

I warmed to Judy, as we talked for over an hour on the phone. I suggested that I travel down to Cornwall, visit her Flicka Foundation, get a view and perspective of what I thought she needed and see if I could help.

The Flicka Foundation was a very effective, attractive charity which was involved in some wonderful work with both rescuing horses and donkeys. It was in a lovely spot overlooking the sea and Falmouth harbour. I could see immediately that they had a lot of donkeys and not an awful lot of room. As Judy explained, the council and relevant dignitaries had not rushed to their aid or their quest to enlarge and expand the project.

There were not enough things to attract the public, of most importance, no brown signs to let everyone know where they actually were.

I spent a day at Flicka as the journey is a little too long to go there and back in a day, but I spent enough time for it to register and to understand the fundamental problems they faced.

Arriving home, I couldn't get out of my mind that there was an association here that we might be able to combine the two. However, it was fraught with difficulties and mandate problems with the Charity Commission, as basically, we didn't actually have the same aims: we focused more on the special needs side, whereas Flicka were hell-bent on the rescue side of things and to give a home or re-home the animals, if possible.

So, I thought, if we couldn't bring the association together, this might be the time to consider my way out. We could achieve this by closing down my sanctuary, moving all my donkeys down to Cornwall, let Flicka take over the strain and the work, leaving me to fundraise and make that side work as a success for them, alleviating their concerns for the future which was so evidently hanging over their heads, like a noose.

After a year of trials and tribulations, I did just that. We sold the farm and I made numerous journeys in a lorry to Cornwall, making sure they got every fence post, all the railings, saddles, bridles, tearoom chairs, and tables, everything that we had accumulated over twenty-nine years. At the end of those journeys, it was time to get the donkeys down which was done successfully, in four large horse boxes.

The donkeys immediately responded well to their new surroundings, making friends with the hundred or so donkeys that had been there for some time. Everything worked well. We were able to fight for and gain the farmhouse sale and give the proceeds to the foundation, so they had enough funds to take the extra animals that they had offered this wonderful home to. Also, the money took the financial pressure off them for a few years while everything sorted itself out.

Annie and I enjoy our visits. As time goes by, the donkeys recognise us a little less which we feel sad about but totally understand. We are always sad when Judy has to inform us that one of our beloved animals has passed away. We grieve for not being able to be there for our very special friends to pacify them and spend the last hours in their company which meant so much to us and our existence. To be totally honest, we miss them terribly and our way of life we shared together. They were true and humble friends, incomparable to anything else.

On getting home, we set about starting our new life. Down-sizing into our bungalow which we find cosy and comfortable after an eight-bedroom farmhouse with children running all over the place with a small garden which Annie has turned into an exhibition of outstanding beauty, an entry for Gardeners' World if ever there was one. But we are rarely at home nowadays, as the talks get established and the journeys get longer. My talk, although about my stage and television career, always finishes about the donkeys. The last quarter of an hour is dedicated to those I have absolutely no wish to forget. The money we make goes, in part, to Flicka and we have achieved our goal on that score. Also, the audience around the country seem to be receptive to a dual career, they often find the donkeys more important than the artistic side which is gratifying in so many ways. I am able to enforce the truth about the cruelty still placed on these lovely animals and the situations they get into which is, in most part, not discussed or broached upon. At the same time and very pleasurably, I am able to remember my family publicly and all they did, to keep their immense talent and contribution to the stage, film and television alive. How many of us can do that and enjoy the response so much?

The Flicka Foundation is going strong with more rescues. More grounds have been bought. Two more big barns have been built and we are now in the midst of building an animal hospital which is so vital to organisations like this, so all is well.

Acknowledgements

I would like very much to take this opportunity of thanking all the wonderful groups I have had the pleasure of presenting my *Toytown to Buckingham Palace* night to over the past three years.

My appreciation, recognition and respect goes to all the individual branches and county Federation conferences where I have delivered my talk and to the branches where I have completed auditions too.

I find it a joy to entertain and to be in the company of groups, both large and small, intimate or large, every evening is different, there's always something to relate to, gather or just enjoy. We have a party, let's hope it continues for as long as I can stand up and the ladies still want me. It is the most wonderful organisation and one to be cherished and treated with respect and admiration.

The whole experience has been and continues to be not only a massive privilege and a huge enjoyment but also on many occasions inspirational, so thank you ladies.

Disclaimers

Please note that many of the names of the participants in the WI branches mentioned in the chapters above and appendices below have been changed to protect the privacy of the individuals concerned.

Also, a small amount of poetic licence has been employed in enhancing some of the humorous aspects of the story.

Appendices

Letters of thanks from various WI's

Letter from Dunchurch and Thurlaston WI (ch.6)

Jennifer Pratt
Vice President
Dunchurch and Thurlaston WI

Dear John and Annie,

I am writing on behalf of the Dunchurch and Thurlaston WI to thank you both for entertaining us so royally at our June meeting.

It was a fascinating talk, so many of our members could relate to the many famous and fondly remembered names of earlier years with whom you were associated.

Needless to say, how you kept going through all the things that happened on the evening was unbelievable, although I know our committee were asking you to carry on, how you did it, we find astonishing.

Needless to say, your tireless work to establish your donkey sanctuary struck a chord with our ladies and we wish you both and especially Annie, with what was a traumatic finale, our very best wishes and a continuing success in the future.

Jennifer Pratt
Vice President

PS We understand the medics had a good night too.

Correspondence relating to Phoebe and Baz (ch. 7)

Dear John and Annie,

In my attempt to be positive, I am writing to you, firstly in thanks that show no boundaries for all you both have done over the years for both Phoebe but also for her school over the past few years. I cannot begin to describe the children's' pleasure and excitement that they have derived from their visits and their therapeutic pleasure and excitement that they have derived from their visits and their therapeutic weekends with you both and your wonderful words. The sight of the donkeys always made all the problems, trials and tribulations just fade away.

You were both so attentive to Phoebe when she came and while Annie was showing all the other children around the meadows and fields, you always stayed back with her and always managed to make her feel very special, which indeed she was.

We visited finally at a time when you were preparing for a long and arduous walk, we could see the pressures you were both under and yet, there was Phoebe and you dropped everything for her monthly visit that meant the world to her. That day, I think your instincts kicked in, you noticed that Phoebe was not her usual self. She was fighting but gently losing the battle. You gave her a large, funny replica of Baz and you whispered to her that now she could take Baz home with her.

That furry donkey never left her side when she could no longer come to you, I cannot describe efficiently her delight when you brought the real Baz over to the Hospice to say a proper goodbye.

'Lil', as Phoebe called her had five collars, one for daytime, one for night-time, one for breakfast and one for tea-time and even the last one was only for Sundays, that little cuddly donkey was an enormous comfort to her and she loved it dearly.

Sadly, as you know, Phoebe passed away on Tuesday the 3rd of June, unable to fight the pneumonia which the muscular dystrophy could not resist. Her mother expressed a wish that Phoebe should take the donkey with her which she most definitely wanted to do, we thought that was right, as they were inseparable in life, so they should be in death. I hope this doesn't make you both feel too sad as it is a mark of friendship. Baz was a true friend to Phoebe and someone in her mind to care for, which she could manage in her own way. We gained comfort from the joy it bought this very bright and intelligent child and the hope and the pleasure she also got from her visits.

Our thanks to you both always.

Emily Cronan – Phoebe's carer and friend

Dear Emily,

Thank you so much for your letter. Far from feeling sad, I am filled with warmth that we could have been just very small part of a wonderful child's life. I am also filled with respect and admiration for the work you did over such a long period of time and our small gesture fades into obscurity when one considers the twenty-four hour love and care you gave that child, always smiling and always trying to make Phoebe's life have meaning and filled the time you had together with such affection.

Perhaps it is not for me to make you aware that Baz too, passed away in September not that long after Phoebe. He was thirty-seven, a good age for a donkey, so now they are once again most definitely back together again in a much more suitable place enjoying much happier times together.

Love to you,

John and Annie

Appraisal from the Bookham Belles (ch.10)

From Toytown to Buckingham Palace

The Bookham Belles

September 24th, 2017

After the Summer break, the Belles came out in force for our first meeting of the Autumn and no words can describe how wonderful our evening was mainly due to our amazing speaker.

John Stirling came all the way from Manchester with his wife Annie to tell us his story, *Toytown to Buckingham Palace*.

The hall was filled with laughter and tears and pure astonishment at John's extraordinary career as a child actor, producer, director and playwright.

He started as Noddy on the West End stage, worked with the likes of Jimmy Edwards in *Whack-O*, with Jack Warner of *Dixon of Dock Green* fame and Sid James before spending six years alongside Morecambe and Wise. He produced several Royal Variety Performances, wrote a musical for Marti Caine and even wrote a special play for Patricia Hayes. This lead him on to the next chapter in his life, rescuing donkeys.

John and his wife Annie, who was a costume designer for many TV series like *Sunday Night at the London Palladium* to *Stars in Your Eyes* and many others, set up an inspirational charity with Dame Judi

Dench, rescuing donkeys, creating a wonderful environment for them and training them to work with special needs children. Through this work, they came into contact with many other famous actors, June Brown, Edward Fox, Brian Blessed and even Her Majesty the Queen.

Following his entertaining talk, one that the Belles said was the best ever, John signed books and Annie sold beautiful toy donkeys and donkey-themed aprons all the proceeds going to provide much needed services and support for children.

As the Belles swarmed their tables, buying up every donkey in sight, refreshments were served, and the socialising commenced!

There was a general consensus that we were so glad as we assisted in removing the bell at Betchworth otherwise we would never had had the most wonderful evening in the company of such a wonderful couple.

President of the Bookham Belles

E-mail from Thurston WI (ch.17)

Dear John,

What an absolutely splendid evening last night, enjoyed by all and straight off the top of your head, how well the two of you work together, very positive.

Thank you also this morning from our groups of WI's, one describing you as a real showman to the core.

John, I was so pleased you were able to come.

The very best wishes to you both,

Sarah Robinson
Thurston WI

Report from Thedwastre Group of WI's (ch.17)

Thedwastre Group Meeting

Hosted by Thurston WI, the annual general meeting of the Thedwastre Group took place on the 16th October at the New Green centre, Thurston, Bury St. Edmunds.

Following *Jerusalem*, the presidents of participating institutes introduced themselves and gave an account of the highlights of their year's activities which included a huge variety of events, talks, fund raising, trips and visits.

The highlight of the evening was the talk by John Stirling, who made a colourful entrance in a long, oversized cardigan which suggested that his talk was going to be fun. He spoke about his childhood from being expelled from boarding school to being sent to the Italia Conti Stage School at the age of nine.

Playing Noddy in the West End, having been chosen to so be so by Enid Blyton herself. Eighty-two episodes of *Whack-o* with Jimmy Edwards and four hundred television appearances as a child actor, completely astounded the audience. At the age of fourteen, he joined the BBC's radio repertory company and performed in shows like *Ray's a Laugh* where he met Patricia Hayes who remained a close friend for many years. He became a producer working with Morecambe and Wise, Billy Fury, even the Beatles.

The friends and colleagues from show business have been paramount in the success of John's second passion providing refuge for donkeys at the sanctuary he and his wife built alongside Dame Judi Dench and June Brown who received an MBE for her involvement.

John and his wife work tirelessly with the donkeys to raise awareness of the plight of some of these animals and to help raise funds for their rescue and care for the work they do with special children who need the therapy. This has included very long walks the first when Annie walked from Derbyshire to Assisi in Northern Italy with her donkey Beethoven to visit the patron saint of all animals St. Francis. Subsequently, Annie went from Balmoral Castle to Buckingham Palace with her donkey, walking all the way, resulting in a private audience with the Queen.

After his inspiring performance, he spent a good while with all the women who wanted to share with him the memories and nostalgia he had brought to the evening.

An excellent evening Thurston.

Valerie Ford
Programme Secretary

Update from Menai Straits WI (ch.24)

From Sharon Crowden

Programme organiser – Menai Straits WI

We were contacted by John himself, offering his services to come and speak to us at our WI on his subject, *Toytown to Buckingham Palace*. I must admit I was intrigued from his e-mail and googled him. I discovered that he lived in Derbyshire, so I replied to him, making our apologies that it was doubtful we could cover his travelling expenses and was he aware that we were in North Wales?

He replied very promptly that yes, he was aware and he and his wife love to visit Anglesey when they can and of course, he would love to come.

We arranged for John, his wife and a whole herd of donkeys to be the speaker at our Christmas meeting in St. Anne's meeting room at the Catholic church in Menai Bridge.

John had been in North Wales a couple of weeks previously and met up with our president, Glynne Owen, just to finalise things and make sure he knew where we met.

We opened the evening to members and their friends too, so had a really good turn-out on the night. John and Annie arrived in plenty of time, with a lot of gear to set up. From the title of his talk, we really had no idea what to expect, but John soon had us in stitches with tales of his birth and early childhood (when he was kept a secret by his beautiful mother), star-struck by mention of the big stars he had worked with   (Morecambe and Wise, Judi Dench, Brian Blessed), and impressed by his and his wife's tireless work with their donkey sanctuary and work with children with special needs.

John kept us well entertained with his stories and pictures, aided by the lovely Annie. We were all so interested in Annie's fundraising by trekking so many miles with donkeys and all the kindness and hospitality of other WI groups offering warm beds and food to keep her going.

It was a fabulous evening and we thoroughly enjoyed his company. We all bought Annie's furry donkeys to remember them both by.

Author's career

Writer, director and producer, John Stirling has a significant body of work completed over many years;

Once in a Lifetime – Musical starring Marti Caine for both theatre and BBC television.

Gert and Daisy – Musical starring Sylvia Simms and Rosemary Leach for theatre and television.

Gert and Daisy – Musical starring Rosemary Leach and Josephine Tewson for BBC television.

Overture and Beginners – Musical starring Michel Le Grand, Sacha Distel, Jane Lapotaire for both theatre and BBC television.

Donezetti – Masterclass starring June Brown and the Covent Garden Orchestra for theatre and BBC television.

Marked for Life – Drama starring Patricia Hayes for BBC television.

The Clattering of the Clogs – Drama starring Brian and Micheal for theatre and BBC television.

Lowrie the Concert – Starring Betty Driver for theatre and BBC television's Blue Peter.

Cheers Mrs Worthington – Musical starring Diana Coupland and Charlie Drake for theatre and London Weekend Television.

Simon – Musical at the Theatre Royal, Drury Lane and London Weekend Television.

Not One Bray goes by – Drama starring June Brown for theatre and BBC television.

To Tina with Love – Televised charity concert at the Theatre Royal, Drury Lane.

Once in a Lifetime – Starring John Noakes, Peter Purves and Lesley Judd for theatre and television.

Position's held;

Part of Granada's Televisions Production team for 7 years.

Talent Co-ordinator at London Weekend Television for 4 years.

Royal Variety Show for 3 years.

Michael Elliot Trust Awards Night for 6 years.

Latest work;

Born in a Hamper – Drama for theatre and television (touring).

Toytown to Buckingham Palace – John Stirling is a popular and sought-after after-dinner speaker with a number of prominent organisations.